DAWN OVER BAGHDAD

DAWN
OVER BAGHDAD

How the U.S. Military Is Using
Bullets and Ballots to Remake Iraq

KARL ZINSMEISTER

ENCOUNTER BOOKS
SAN FRANCISCO

First edition published in 2004 by Encounter Books, an activity of Encounter for Culture and Education, Inc., a nonprofit, tax exempt corporation.

Encounter Books website address: www.encounterbooks.com

Manufactured in the United States and printed on acid-free paper.

The paper used in this publication meets the minimum requirements of ANSI/NISO Z39.48-1992 (R 1997)(*Permanence of Paper*).

FIRST EDITION

Library of Congress Cataloging-in-Publication Data

Zinsmeister, Karl.
  Dawn over Baghdad : how the U.S. military is using bullets and ballots to remake Iraq / Karl Zinsmeister.
      p.   cm.
    ISBN 1-59403-050-2 (alk. paper)
    1. Iraq War, 2003.   2. Democracy—Iraq.   3. Iraq War, 2003—Reconstruction.   4. Iraq War, 2003—Mass media and the war.   I. Title.
  DS79.76 .Z565 2004
  956.7044'3—dc22

                                                        2004047184

10   9   8   7   6   5   4   3   2

To Chris and David,
for my chance

When winter threatens,
Think of the faith of the crocus.
When war rages,
Think of the heart of the hero.
—Diane Strader

CONTENTS

All the photographs in this book were taken in Iraq by the author.

Introduction

AMERICA'S WARRIOR CLASS

Most of this book is careful eyewitness narration of a story that has been inadequately covered by the major media: the unfolding of the guerilla war, counterinsurgency and reconstruction in Iraq. But before turning to more objective reporting on current events, I'd like to introduce readers to some of the U.S. military men and women I met in the course of my work as an embedded journalist. Having spent many weeks living and operating with soldiers in the combat zones of the Middle East during 2003 and 2004, let me say simply that there are some families in this country to whom the rest of us owe a great deal.

Take, for example, the clan of Sean Shields, the young American I photographed in combat in Samawah for the cover of *Boots on the Ground,* my previous book about the spring hot war in Iraq. Lieutenant Shields, a black-haired Pennsylvania college wrestler, is the third generation of his family to serve in the U.S. Army airborne corps. Sean's grandfather Robert was one of the men who established the stellar reputation of the 82nd Airborne Division during World

War II by parachuting into Normandy, then later Nijmegen, and fighting fiercely against the German army. For his leadership during the Battle of the Bulge, he was lifted from the enlisted ranks directly into the officer corps.

At Normandy, the elder Shields jumped in pitch black, and there were no night-vision goggles in those days. As he reached the ground, his parachute snagged on a tree and he swung hard into the side of a stone building; he was knocked out cold and hung there for an unknown period of time. When he came to, still dangling in the air, he cut himself free from his parachute harness and fell to the ground. In the dark, he promptly stumbled into a foxhole of German soldiers, losing his Thompson submachine gun in the process. So his introduction to Normandy began with a knife fight. Which he won.

Grandpa Shields, incidentally, is still working today, at age eighty-three, for the Rockland County Sheriff's Department in New York State. His son, Sean's father, also became a paratrooper, served in Gulf War I, and eventually retired as a colonel. Now Sean is an Army Ranger in the 82nd Airborne, and has just returned from a year of service in Iraq, where I spent time with him on two different occasions. In the course of doing his share of the dirty work in Samawah and Baghdad and points in between, Sean was blasted twice by roadside bombs. He shook off both attacks.

TROOPER TALENT

Quite apart from the bravery and dedication many of them exhibit, the people currently serving in our military display a far wider range of talents than most Americans appreciate. In my months of observing our fighting forces in action, I've come across suburbanites, hillbillies, street kids from concrete canyons, trust fund babies, farmboys, computer nerds, theater directors, quarterbacks and much more. Columbia University professor Hamid Dabashi was quite wrong about the faculties of average soldiers today when he praised a group of Iraq war protesters for being "'A' students, who think for themselves," in contrast to the "'C' students with their stupid fingers on the trigger." I've spent time with numerous soldiers who are graduates of tony schools like Wesleyan, Cornell and Vassar—not only in the officer corps but in the ranks. I've met disciplined immigrants from Colombia, Russia, Panama and other countries. I've observed flocks of high-tech aces and mechanical whizzes who keep our battlefield computers, helicopters and radars humming.

One of the battalion commanders I became acquainted with over the last year was assigned a driver who has a master's degree and a CPA certification. Lieutenant Colonel Dave Haight joked with the soldier that "it's not a good thing for an officer's driver to be smarter than he is." Then he asked what drew the young man into the Army. "I'm gonna have lots of years to make money," came the answer. "I wanted to make sure I did one thing in my life that really made a difference."

I know of a man, Steve Chesser, who was most of the way through a Ph.D. program at Fordham University when, looking for a more active and patriotic career, he decided he'd like to start jumping out of perfectly good airplanes with the 82nd Airborne. He entered not as an officer but as a private. When I met him four years later, he was a highly competent sergeant.

I shared a tent with a soldier who, after suddenly breaking into fluent Spanish, explained that he had picked up the language while serving as a missionary in South America for three years before joining the Army. This mature and worldly individual was a rank-and-file paratrooper.

Another entry-level soldier from California whom I got to know was, if I had to guess, probably not a stellar book learner. But after just a few minutes of conversation I could tell he had a quick native intelligence and was a classic American autodidact. He had trained himself in German, thinking it might aid his aspiration to enter the Special Forces, and on his own time was now studying battlefield medicine. Envisioning some sort of advanced first aid, I discovered to my surprise that he had recently taught himself how to do emergency tracheotomies.

A military translator I met had recently finished learning one of the world's hardest languages—Mandarin—when the Army, noting his verbal facility, asked him to become an Arabic speaker. So he went right back to school to master another of the planet's hardest languages. This man's intellectual ability would make him a success in any number of fields, but he has chosen to serve his country as a multilingual sergeant. "Don't ask," he replied wearily when I asked him what language he dreams in.

Every time I rub shoulders with members of our Army, I meet individuals like these who possess quirky talents and a taste for stiff challenges. While re-embedded with troops in the Sunni Triangle in January 2004, I bumped into soldiers ranging from a New York City reservist with a business degree from Oxford University who is now running a business incubator in Baghdad for the Army, to the 2002 quarterback of the Army football team (Chad Jenkins), currently a lieutenant directing combat operations with the 10th Mountain Division.

I spent several days with Captain Chris Cirino, a quick-tongued blond with a biting sense of humor who was born in 1967. "I grew up on Long Island in an upper-middle-class household," he told me. "My dad ran libraries and my mom was a professor of French. But I was a troubled student. Not evil or stupid, just restless and undisciplined. I was basically expelled from high school in the last week of my senior year, so I never got a degree." He joined the Army at age seventeen.

"I put in a tour and found I liked it. It helped me pull myself together. Among other things I got a GED, and then left the service to go to college. I majored in Asian studies, with a minor in Korean history, and decided to just keep working right through summers and college breaks. So I ended up coming out after four years with both a B.A. and a master's degree. I like to tell people I may be the only person they'll ever meet with both a GED and a master's."

At that point, Cirino realized he missed military service. "But if you leave the Army for more than a few months and then come back they make you start again at the bottom.

So even though I'd been discharged as a sergeant and then acquired a lot of education, I was back in as a lowly specialist, and had to re-do basic training. But one of the instructors there picked me out and recommended me for Officer Candidate School. So in 1994 I jumped from the enlisted ranks into an eventual position as a second lieutenant.

"I went back to Korea in 1995, then spent a couple of years in the 1st Ranger Battalion. I met lots of guys kind of like me there. My platoon had a lawyer, two experienced teachers, and an accountant. Guys who just didn't want to be shut up in offices.

"I became the head of mountaineering instruction at the Army Ranger School. Then I became a rifle company commander with the 82nd. And now I'm this battalion's headquarters company commander."

YES MEN, NO

Our soldiers aren't all saints and scholars, but they're a good cross-section of America, and the base of our military pyramid is chock full of impressive people. There are also many talented men and women at the middle and top of the command structure. The commanders who led U.S. Army divisions during the first year of guerilla war in Iraq are instructive examples.

Brigadier General Martin Dempsey, who heads the 1st Armored Division in Baghdad, has earned, in addition to his military achievements, three separate master's degrees, including one in English from Duke. Major General David Petraeus, who guided the soldiers of the 101st Airborne as they restarted civilization in northern Iraq, was well equipped for that task thanks to, among other credentials, a Ph.D. in international relations from Princeton (which he earned two years faster than most doctoral candidates). The commander of our third full division in Iraq during the guerilla war, Major General Raymond Odierno of the 4th Infantry Division, has a master's in nuclear engineering, and is known equally for his brilliance and for his fighting prowess.

These smart, competent soldiers and officers are essential to America's new style of fighting—which can be likened to chess, by contrast with the "checkers" style of combat (much slower, less mobile, more ponderous) that was practiced as recently as the first Gulf War. Far more than in the past, today's servicemen must think and adapt on the fly. The speed of maneuver and pace of battle have ratcheted up dramatically, and complex equipment and tactics must be brought to bear. In place of the sheer mass of force they once relied upon, our military units are substituting superior mobility, intelligence and precision.

Of course, this formula works only if there are bright, flexible, independent people behind the wheels of the vehicles, at the eyepieces of the scopes and on the triggers of the weapons. Discussions of our nation's warfighting abilities often center on the computerized technologies and needle-nosed weapons we bring to the battlefield. But smart, tough battlefield decision-makers, much more than the advanced technologies themselves, are the key to the superiority of today's American military.

One of my favorite combat photographs from those I've taken in Iraq is a shot of a bright young soldier in his early twenties named Josh Farley. He's standing, with his fingers on the red firing buttons, at the sight of a quarter-million-dollar TOW missile launcher, a potent high-tech weapon; but right in front of him is a "Grilled Beefsteak" MRE, and next to him is one of the water bottles the soldiers lugged everywhere to keep themselves alive in the deserts of Iraq. Here, I concluded after observing weeks of battle, are the real essentials that make the U.S. military so formidable: not the fancy gear, but the dedicated soldiers equipped with whatever basics are necessary to keep them in the fight.

The American industrialist Andrew Carnegie once proclaimed that if you snatched away his workers and left behind his world-beating factories, there would be grass growing in the cracks of their floors within six months, but if you removed his factories and left his workers, in six months those men and women would have built new and better factories. After watching them fight in Iraq, that's exactly my view of America's fighting forces. You could take all of their leading-edge equipment and technology and every penny of the large sums we devote to national defense, and hand it all to some competing nation, and they would not be able to create a force as effective as our current military—because they would not have the self-reliant, resourceful, adapt-and-go American soldiers, sailors, airmen and Marines who bring these weapons to bear with such competence.

Independent thinking by line soldiers is not only tolerated in our armed forces, it is *required* by the new freelancing style of warfare. Outsiders who envision our armed services as authoritarian institutions would be quite surprised to learn how much less they rely on orders from above than on problem-solving by small units. Our military is highly meritocratic, and obstacles are generally surmounted after open contention among competing views. I've witnessed many spirited debates—both among officers in the command tents and between privates and sergeants at the base of the military pyramid—over the best ways to achieve important objectives. The general *modus operandi* is competition: "May the smartest idea and biggest biceps win."

While they are highly disciplined, our elite military outfits are also surprisingly open and democratic, with little evidence of intimidation or the "yes man" syndrome. In my previous book I described walking into a bathroom in a military camp one night to find the 82nd's brigade commander—a man with life-and-death authority over nearly four thousand men—scrubbing his dirty socks and underwear in a bucket, just like any good private. How many college deans or corporate executives or newspaper publishers are as egalitarian?

CITIZEN SOLDIERS

So: America's current soldiers are skilled enough to fly missiles into specific windows, squeeze off one-mile sniper shots, and negotiate subtly with local leaders (actual events I witnessed in Iraq). And most of them are fine citizen-representatives of our open and democratic society. They are also interesting on a third front: for their decency and idealism.

Hollywood war stories like *Saving Private Ryan* and *Black Hawk Down* have widely promulgated the idea that contemporary soldiers fight not for cause or country but simply for the survival of themselves and their buddies. I can report that this is emphatically untrue of the American soldiers in Iraq. I found them to be quite conscious of the titanic clash of moral universes that lies behind today's U.S. venture into the Middle East. Most are not only aware of the historic importance of this fight, but quite proud of their role in it; they are broadly motivated by high principles extending far beyond self-preservation.

I know numerous soldiers who put aside well-paying jobs, family life, graduate school or comfortable careers after the September 11 attacks—having concluded that their country needed their military service. I think of Kyle Kissinger, the son of an engineer and a nursing supervisor, who had glided through gifted-student programs before landing a high-paying job as an open-heart surgery technician. Then 9/11 convinced him that his nation had more important work. He is now a medic in the 82nd Airborne, hoping for an eventual career as an Army doctor.

During my very latest stint in Iraq, I encountered a Los Angeles police officer who enlisted right after September 11. In Baghdad I met a soldier I'd first crossed paths with nine months earlier during the spring invasion—Gregory Kolodciejczky, a strapping, blond Pole known as "Special K" to his buddies. He immigrated to the Greenpoint neighborhood in Brooklyn as a teen, and had been a New York City fire marshal. When the Twin Towers went down, fourteen men from his local stationhouse were killed. He vowed to help make sure the events of that day would never be replayed in his adopted country. At age thirty-two he chucked everything and embarked on a new career as a paratrooper. Kolodciejczky believes that by fighting in Iraq he is honoring the memory of his dead friends, and helping to protect Americans like his young daughter from future acts of terror.

It was also idealism that brought Chris Cirino back into the Army after he had completed his master's degree. "I had gone completely through the process to join the Secret Service. Then, in the first week of October 1993, I read a *Newsweek* article about the firefight in Somalia which cost Gary Gordon and Randy Shughart their lives, and won them posthumous Medals of Honor. I had known those guys a little bit in Korea, and the bravery and self-lessness of their actions really moved me. So I re-enlisted."

■ ■

The American patriot Thomas Paine once said, "If there must be trouble, let it be in my day, so that my children may have peace." That is a creed many our soldiers hold to quite literally. The deployed GIs I have asked tell me they don't want any waffling or hesitation about finishing the job in Iraq. Some of these men were there in 1991; they want a conclusive victory this time so they won't need to come back again. They say it is much less important that the Iraqi war be over soon than that it be successful, and they know it will take time.

Last fall while I was in Dallas for a nationwide radio interview, the sister of an 82nd soldier called in to the station to read one of his letters on the air. In it, he commented with great satisfaction on the absence of terrorist attacks in the United States itself in the time since our military went to Afghanistan and Iraq. That, he said, is exactly what our armed services are for—to deflect the pain of fighting from our homeland, transfer it to the enemy's backyard, and ultimately put an end to it. Easy for us to say from our armchairs; quite a noble sentiment from a man writing from the midst of battle in the Sunni Triangle.

Families of some of the soldiers I've reported on have mailed me copies of their letters home, and many of these reflect other kinds of American idealism. During the long, hot Iraqi summer of 2003, Lieutenant John Gibson of the 82nd's 325th Regiment wrote his mom and dad on his birthday to report,

> We are homesick and want to see our families and loved ones, but not at the expense of an incomplete mission. I know that a completely free and democratic Iraq may not be in place by the time that I leave, but it will be significantly under way before I am redeployed. I see things here, on a daily basis, that hurt the human heart. I see poverty, crime, terrorism, murder, and stupidity. However I see hope in the eyes of many Iraqis, hope for a chance to govern themselves. I think they are on the cusp of a new adventure, a chance for an entire country to start over again."

Private Melville Johnson reflected on his time in combat this way:

> In the city of Samawah my battalion engaged in the hottest firefight the division has been in since Vietnam. Every paratrooper who fought in that battle fought bravely and honorably. The day after the battle, we took

positions in the streets among the blown-out buildings. One by one the people returned. The adults set commerce in motion. The laughter and splashing of children playing in the Euphrates was a great relief to hear. Every day I was blessed with kind words of gratitude.

I feel Iraq has real potential for the future—with the help of the U.S. military, humanitarian agencies, and the installation of a just, fair, and compassionate government. I feel tremendously for the American families that lost a loved one. I also feel for the families of the enemy. At night, before I rest, I think of the enemy we killed. I remember the way their bodies lay in unnatural states, positions God never intended them to take. I hope these images will soon fade.

Would I willingly, happily, and completely fight this war again? Yes. I would do it all over again with just as much, or more, determination.

MILITARY CULTURE

In a brilliant essay penned shortly after 9/11, my friend Fred Turner wrote that "American military prowess comes not from a militaristic society. It comes from a depth of culture and a density of history, from a constant striving for goodness." In a practical sense, Fred is agreeing with Victor Davis Hanson's statement, in another fine essay, that "We are militarily strong because of our culture. When it comes to war, 1 billion people and the world's oil are not nearly as valuable military assets as MIT, West Point, the U.S. House of Representatives, C-SPAN, Bill O'Reilly, and the GI Bill."

But I think Fred is also arguing that America's fighting forces are so potent because of what America's best soldiers carry inside them. Shortly after the Titanic sunk, one of the New York City newspapers ran a matched pair of photos. One was captioned "Nature's Power over Man," and showed the great ship slipping under the waves. The other photo was labeled "Man's Power over Nature." It showed a man handing his life jacket to a woman. On that vessel where life jackets were in grossly short supply, that man undoubtedly died. So in what sense was he triumphing over anything? In the sense that he demonstrated the capacity of humans to rise above their animal selfishness and do something higher, purer and more permanent than merely sustaining their own life.

Turner notes that American society has a fashionable, amoral, selfish layer at its surface

> that conceals a great enduring American heartland beneath.... Foreigners acquainted only with our Hollywood narcissism, TV sex, artistic trash, and academic twaddle can easily mistake us as morally flabby and unable to defend ourselves: ripe pickings for the samurai or mujahideen of a more determined culture.

But beneath this surface is a more formidable America

> that exists quietly between our coasts. And not only the geographic heartland of small-town America has this deep strength. New York City surprised everybody after September 11 with its courage, resilience, spirit of fraternity, and spontaneous patriotism and faith in God. Our heartland is everywhere: in the firehouses of Man-

hattan, in the business people who meet the payroll, in the honest reporters of the press.

It was this America, says Turner, that

> defeated the most powerful nation on earth to get its independence, that fought the battle of Gettysburg with *itself* over matters of principle, the nation that smashed the Japanese Imperial Navy at Midway, and that outlasted the cruelest and most well-armed empire in the world in the Cold War. A nation slow to anger, but hazardous when roused and deadly patient when necessary; the only way to escape its just wrath is to seek its forgiveness—which is, admittedly, always immediate and generous.

In a book that complements Turner's argument nicely, foreign policy scholar Walter Mead suggests that the secret to U.S. international strength is the moral fiber of ordinary Americans. Principles "of honor, independence, courage, and military pride" are "deeply embedded" in average citizens. Folk traditions of "implacable determination to defend the American way of life, regardless of cost," and "the view that when you fight, it must be to win—no holds barred" are the things that have kept our country free and strong over three centuries.

When U.S. Army General Order No. 11 created the first Memorial Day, it referred to everyday Americans "who made their breasts a barricade between our country and its foes." Across many episodes of American history, that has been a fairly literal encapsulation of events. And it's still true today.

During quiet periods in our national history, when citizens turn more materialistic and inward, it's easy for cynics to scoff at "sentimental" notions of courage and patriotism like these. But when homicidal fanatics bring death to our door, there are always Americans who step outside to greet them. That is not a jingoistic fantasy but a fact—and a very fortunate one for our nation.

■ ■

When I speak to audiences, I sometimes run into individuals who assume that our soldiers in Iraq must be having a hard time keeping their morale and fighting spirit up, given the tough physical conditions and unpredictable attacks of the guerilla war. They ask whether our service members feel discouraged or taken advantage of. I tell them I can only report that the individuals I observed in combat for over a quarter of the year were, as a group, amazingly spirited and unbowed.

Some people—particularly intellectuals and literary folk—forget that there are certain men whose reflex is literally to run *into* danger, rather than away from it. These are the men who become police officers and firemen—or soldiers. They know their work is perilous and they don't want to be injured; but if they were concerned primarily about safety, they would have become chefs or graduate students, not GIs. Chasing down bad guys provides them with a deep sense of satisfaction that is often lost on outside observers.

I once attended a conference with a group of academics and journalists at the Cantigny estate outside Chicago, which is also home to one of the finer military museums in the country. During a lunch break I toured the exhibits, and when I came back I told a professor and a reporter about the extraordinary actions of a World War I soldier catalogued in the museum. This infantryman, just out of the hospital from an earlier bayoneting, was attacking German lines during the Battle of Soissons when the explosion of an artillery shell dislodged some timbers and pinned his arm where he lay by the top of a trench, crushing it badly. As eight German soldiers ran toward him, he managed to shoot four of them down with his .45 caliber sidearm, then take the other four prisoner. Before they realized he was trapped, he had disarmed them. Then he removed his belt, applied it to his arm as a tourniquet, and used his bayonet to cut off his own crushed limb so he would be able to escape. He was crossing back to American lines holding his four prisoners at one-armed gunpoint when another shell burst, killing one of the Germans and breaking the American's leg. Still clutching his .45, the GI ordered the remaining prisoners to carry him the rest of the way to a U.S. trench.

After I'd relayed these details, the journalist burst out with "yeah, right, in which cartoon did this take place?" I admitted it was a remarkable story, but said these were the actual deeds of a real American soldier. The two conference-goers refused to believe anyone could be capable of these acts. But there really was such a man; his name was Dan Edwards, and for his achievements he was awarded the Medal of Honor in 1918.

While journalists and academics may think it fantasy, men capable of finding the strength to do such things truly do exist. After the phony attributions of heroism to Jessica Lynch and the sour soap opera that followed, I must note that since the war in Iraq commenced, many U.S. soldiers have displayed genuine self-sacrificial bravery. Like 82nd Airborne medic Alan Babin, who left a covered position and exposed himself on the battlefield to come to the aid of another soldier. He was shot in the abdomen and is now fighting his way back from the loss of numerous organs, several full-body arrests, and more than twenty operations. Or Sergeant Andrew Baddick, who was on night patrol near Abu Ghuraib when he saw a Military Police Humvee roll into an irrigation canal, trapping four MPs in twelve feet of fast-flowing water. He stripped off his equipment and dived in to help the struggling men as they were swept downstream. He pulled one soldier, heavily laden with body armor and helmet, to the surface and shoved him up the bank. Told that another MP had sunk underwater, Baddick shouted, "I'll get him!" and dived back in— only to be sucked into a culvert that carried the water underground beneath a highway, where he drowned.

The astonishing thing, when you interview soldiers who have been wounded in action in Iraq, is how many of them volunteer the same thoughts: They don't regret the fight; there was somebody else who was more selfless or brave; and—almost universally—how anxious they are to return to their units.

Where does this sturdiness come from? A letter I received at the end of 2003 from a retired Army officer named Tom Tinsley gives some hints:

> The magic I found in the Army was repeated again and again. Colonels teaching captains ... sergeants teach-

ing privates and specialists. Handing down the tribal wisdom to the following generation. I have been in corporate life for seven years now, and have found nothing like it outside the Army. Leaders unselfishly preparing the next generation, who will in turn pass it on to those who will succeed them.

It's easy for critics on both the left and the right to convince themselves that the United States is a decadent society, that our young people have gone soft, that we will never produce another generation like the men who climbed the cliffs at Normandy on D-day. That judgment, I'm here to report, is as wrong as wrong can be. We've got plenty of soldiers in uniform today whom Americans can trust with any responsibility, any difficulty, any mortal challenge.

In a small church in Leicestershire built during England's disastrous Civil War, there is an inscription over the door that reads: "When all things sacred were throughout the nation demolished or profaned, Sir Richard Shirley, baronet, founded this church. His singular praise it is to have done the best things in the worst times."

To do the best things in the worst times: that's a pretty good description of the aspirations of our fighting men and women in the Middle East. As they continue to endure arduous tests, we give thanks for them.

In what follows, I tell the story of their efforts over the past year to do good in the tormented nation of Iraq—using bullets, ballots, and any other available instrument.

1

CRACKDOWN

In January 2004 I returned to Iraq to be re-embedded with American troops. I'd spent the previous March and April reporting on the offensive against Saddam, so this was my third month in the country out of the past eleven. My purpose this time was to observe combat operations and reconstruction work during the guerilla phase of the war.

On my very first day I was confronted with reminders of how disruptive even a small minority of guerilla fighters can be as this nation tries to mend. When sixty replacement soldiers and I touched down at Baghdad International Airport in a C-130, the receiving tent was filled with agitated men and women whose troop transport had come under rocket fire as they were in the process of flying out. Their departure was aborted with no loss of life or serious injury, but the incident underlines how just a few men with shoulder-launched missiles may be able to keep Iraq's international gateway too dangerous for use by commercial aircraft for some time to come—a reality that hurts Iraq's recovery politically and economically.

Then later in the day, a medical helicopter attached to the 82nd Airborne, the division I would spend most of my time with, was shot down (despite being clearly emblazoned with large red crosses) near Fallujah. All nine people aboard the air ambulance—pilots, medics and injured patients—were killed.

The pressing question faced by American soldiers trying to stabilize Iraq today is how to fight back against such vicious hit-and-run attacks by an obstructionist minority. The straightforward answer is that our fighting forces have to both punish and reward; for winning a guerilla war requires an extremely cagey mix of hard and soft tactics.

■ ■

From the onset of the battles in March 2003 right up to the present moment, U.S. military personnel in Iraq have always tried the humane approach first. In one firefight after another, they have used uncommon care and discrimination, sometimes going to staggering lengths and personal risks to avoid harming innocent civilians and neighborhoods. They did this while killing or capturing thousands of enemy combatants who didn't hesitate to fight from hospitals, schools and family homes.

In *Boots on the Ground,* I argued that the fighting on the way to Baghdad amounted to the gentlest war in history. I described many extraordinary incidents, which I witnessed personally, of disciplined forbearance by American soldiers. This humanitarian concern has been noted by others as well. Reporters for *Time* magazine, for instance, quote an Army sergeant's response to a December 2003 grenade attack that wounded four of his soldiers: "A couple of us saw some guys running away and thought about pulling the trigger. But when you see a guy running through a crowd, do you spray the crowd to get the guy? If, in a situation like that, you can control your impulse for revenge, then that means you are fighting for something bigger."

This temperate, controlled and ethical style of engagement has paid dividends. Ordinary Iraqis took notice of the care with which U.S. soldiers fought. Though most news correspondents have neither noticed nor informed the American public, at the end of the summer, only three out of ten Baghdadis said that American troops had behaved badly during the invasion of their country, while six out of ten thought they had behaved well.* Nationwide research conducted by *The American Enterprise* found that far more Iraqis had a family member, neighbor or friend killed by the security forces of Saddam Hussein than by the 2003 war.

Even during U.S. bombing and ground raids, I have often seen Iraqis continue to shop and travel the streets— because they know American attackers don't kill indiscriminately. If you don't represent a threat, Iraqis recognize, you are pretty safe around the U.S. armed forces. The care with which American fighters have prosecuted their battles is a main reason ordinary Iraqis want nothing to do with the insurgency, and why seven out of ten told *The American Enterprise* and other pollsters in the fall of 2003

---

*Survey by the Gallup Organization.

that they hoped U.S. troops would stay at least another year.

Still, there are limits to the gentle approach.

FIGHTING FIRE WITH FIRE

The minority of Iraqis who resent the ousting of Saddam Hussein are clustered in the so-called Sunni Triangle, where certain villages, cities and neighborhoods have slapped away the American olive branch. During the summer and fall, a few recalcitrant hot spots like Fallujah, Ramadi, Samarra, Balad, Tikrit and parts of Baghdad flamed with guerilla activity. The resistance reached an ugly crescendo around Halloween, when, in one month, eighty-one American soldiers and many Iraqi security personnel and innocent civilians were killed by insurgents operating from these seething niches.

This was when American commanders reached their limit, and all across Iraq the U.S. Army shifted gears. In the first days of November, Generals Charles Swannack (commander of the 82nd Airborne) and John Abizaid (who heads all U.S. military forces in the Middle East) met with sheiks around Fallujah to announce the end of their patience. They made it clear to the assembled Iraqis that after six months of fighting with one hand tied behind their backs, U.S. forces were about to get tough. Unless cooperation from the local populace improved immediately, the region would be squeezed hard.

In other parts of Iraq, Army units launched similar crackdowns. Around Tikrit, the 4th Infantry Division completely ringed in razor wire Saddam's birthplace of Auja, the village of Abu Hishma (a source of many attacks on Americans) and other locales, cutting off these hubs of insurgency from the rest of the country. Buildings that had been used to launch ambushes were shelled or bulldozed. Relatives of wanted insurgency leaders were arrested, questioned and held—a measure that led directly to the capture of Saddam Hussein.

Troops in the Baghdad area launched "Operation Iron Hammer." A series of aggressive raids resulted in a wave of detentions and arms seizures. To end mortar attacks on U.S. bases, commanders initiated "harassment and interdiction" fire—each night, all night, artillery rounds were lobbed preemptively into orchards, fields and abandoned neighborhoods where guerillas had been setting up their mortar tubes. Patrols staked out some of these same places and ambushed would-be ambushers as they gathered.

"Direct-fire attacks on us have dropped dramatically," one soldier told reporter Peter Maas after the program got under way. "We have a pretty clear message. If you shoot at us we will do our damnedest to kill you, and most of the time we will. And if you live in a neighborhood and you know there are bad people and you don't want Americans to return heavy fire into your neighborhood, endangering your families, you need to turn in the bad guys. That message is being received."

Rather than assuming a defensive posture, soldiers took the action to the insurgents. Because Western reporting has concentrated on damage done by guerillas much more than on U.S. countermeasures, few Americans realize how active and successful our soldiers were during the late fall and early winter of 2003. Company commanders out in the neighborhoods, military intelligence specialists interrogating detainees, and CIA and Special Forces teams cultivating informants pressed hard for fresh intelligence, and operations were launched as soon as new information became available. In November and December, U.S. soldiers carried out around 12,000 patrols and 250 raids each and every week. In the process they killed hundreds of enemy fighters, wounded a comparable number and captured thousands.

These get-tough policies quickly bore fruit. The number of guerilla attacks began to fall: from 60-70 daily at the November peak to around 15 per day barely three months later. The U.S. casualty rate tumbled as well. And after Saddam Hussein's arrest on December 13, the violence declined even further.

After a good run of several months (February 2004 was the least deadly month by far since the start of hostilities), the flaring of guerilla attacks around the one-year anniversary of the war brought another bad spike in April. This pattern of two steps forward, one step back is likely to continue for some time.

It is certain that insurgents will do all they can to unsettle the country between now and early 2005, when elections are scheduled. But most of the progress won so far will endure. In Anbar—Iraq's largest province, stretching from Syria almost to Baghdad, covering nearly one-third of the country's land mass and including many of its most restive cities, like Fallujah and Ramadi—it isn't just the reduced number of attacks that encouraged 82nd Airborne Major General Charles Swannack, the local commander.

"More importantly, attacks are increasingly ineffective. Many of the IEDs [Improvised Explosive Device—Army terminology for a hidden roadside bomb] now accurately reflect the title 'improvised.' So recent attacks have been much less effective in terms of injuries and equipment damage." For this, Swannack credits the fact that "we have killed or captured a large number of the leaders, the financiers, and facilitators of the insurgency."

In signals intercepts, interrogations and reports from informants, open discouragement is now being heard from Iraqi intransigents. There are signs in many parts of the country that the insurgency has peaked. In January 2004, for instance, I watched Sunni tribal leaders who had previously refused to sit down with Americans request and receive a reconciliation meeting. "Tips turned in to us for action are up over 50 percent right now," Swannack reports. "About two-thirds of the time we're now receiving tips that tell us exactly where the IEDs are, for example, and we go and dismantle them before we're ever attacked. A lot of good Iraqi people are tired of the violence and want to help the Coalition."

The mix of soft and hard warfighting tactics—always under adjustment, ever varying by time and place—continues to evolve in Iraq. But through trial and error, blending the tactics of carrot and stick, U.S. military and civilian leaders are edging closer to something that Americans since Vietnam have doubted their nation was capable of: the gradual winning of a tough guerilla war.

STRIKE, COUNTERSTRIKE

The war in Iraq is not over. The interval leading up to this summer's handover of power to an interim Iraqi government is a dangerous period when all manner of nihilists and adventurers—homegrown and foreign alike—will do their best to sow fear. Without question, there remains a good deal of dirty work to be carried out in Iraq, and American soldiers and Marines are the ones stepping up to do it.

Each Friday, U.S. soldiers and plainclothes translators are sent out to record the sermons broadcast from many of Iraq's mosques. The tapes are translated and checked for incitements to violence. At 11:45 A.M. on January 2, 2004, two Humvees belonging to Bravo Company of the 2nd Battalion, 325th Regiment, 82nd Airborne set out to monitor one of the forty-four mosques in their battalion's district—a wide swath of southwestern Baghdad. The soldiers in this patrol had been in Iraq for ten months; only sixteen days more and they were scheduled to head back home to the States.

As they approached a sharp bend in a rural road, the second Humvee in line was hit by a powerful roadside bomb (believed to consist of three large artillery shells wired together). The armor-plated vehicle was shredded. Marc Seiden, a popular trooper from New Jersey, took the brunt of the blast in the front passenger seat and was killed instantly. Gunner Solomon Bangayan—who was born and schooled in the Philippines before moving with his family to Vermont—was also killed as he stood exposed in the gun truck's turret. The driver had his arm flayed, and took shrapnel in his throat and neck, but he survived. The fourth soldier was ejected from the vehicle as it rolled, and was pinned under the wreckage for more than an hour before it could be hoisted off his smashed leg.

There's a chance that those involved in planting this particular IED were co-conspirators of the man American soldiers know as Sheik Thoma. Leader of a small mosque just south of where the ambush took place, Thoma (along with some other Sunni clerics) had been preaching a harsh line of anti-American rhetoric to his flock since Saddam's overthrow. Then he made the jump to actually trying to murder Americans himself. On June 14, U.S. soldiers in two vehicles passing through an intersection were astonished to see the imam leap to his feet by the roadside and attempt to launch a rocket at them. A rank amateur in military matters, Thoma was unable to activate the shoulder-fired weapon, and a pair of IEDs that he and two other men had planted failed to explode. The sheik broke into a run, pursued by the soldiers, who soon dragged him to the ground.

When I was with them in the first week of January, the paratroopers who had collared Thoma were preparing to testify against him at trial. Then they learned he had escaped custody, just one day before the proceedings, by crawling under some barbed wire. It was a frustrating loss. Thoma was not only a trigger-puller himself, but also a public figure who incited Iraqis to violence in his poor neighborhood situated within an elbow of the Tigris River. A prize catch—leader of one little piece of the Baghdad anti-American insurgency—had been fumbled away by a careless prison guard. "That's one MP who ought to go to prison himself," more than one paratrooper grumbled.

Soldiers, though, generally don't wring their hands; they act. The response of the battalion in charge of the area in question was to organize a large cordon-and-search mission. Exactly one week after the deaths of infantrymen Seiden and Bangayan, I sit through final planning meetings for Operation Tidal Wave, a sweep by about four thousand paratroopers to take place at dawn on January 11. It is set to commence symbolically with fifteen minutes of aerial bombardment on three sites in this neighborhood from which ambushes have been launched, including the spot where the roadside bomb hit Bravo Company's Humvee—a kind of calling card with the message: "The U.S. remembers what happened here." Then soldiers will flush through the area. Small farms, orchards, mud huts, rural and urban homes will be combed for hidden weapons, for known fugitives like Thoma, and for roadside bombs positioned for future use.

In addition, all men of military age discovered in the area will be gathered into three or four places throughout the morning and subjected to a "collective ass-chewing" (as Lieutenant Colonel Dave Haight calls it). A three-minute message from the 82nd's 2nd Brigade commander will criticize residents for allowing the latest murderous bombing to take place in their neighborhood, explain that no constructive aid or rebuilding projects can be launched until it becomes less dangerous, and warn locals that if resistance continues, the shelling and flood of soldiers seen that morning will be repeated and increased. Printed leaflets will be handed out, and Psychological Operations vehicles equipped with loudspeakers will broadcast the warnings. "The population must see cause and effect between the bad event of January 2 and our physical pressure on their homes," states Lieutenant Colonel Haight at the planning meeting for Operation Tidal Wave.

In addition to the hundreds of routine weekly patrols, meetings, traffic stops, rebuilding projects and raids that the 82nd uses to administer this Al-Rashid region—home to about 1.5 million Baghdadis—several thousand soldiers are mobilized for mass actions of this sort every few weeks. Each time they go, the Iraqi soldiers and policemen that the 82nd has been training play a slightly more prominent role. "This time I want the ICDC [Iraqi Civil Defense Corps] and Iraqi police right out front and center," Haight tells his men. "This is a good chance for residents to see them as a significant force that is going to have to be reckoned with in the future."

SECURITY BLANKET

Nine or ten months after the overthrow of Saddam Hussein, Iraqis were already taking the majority of the casualties from insurgent attacks. This is partly because the security measures set up by American soldiers around critical facilities have been so effective. Baghdad Airport, the halls where the many local democracy councils meet, the camps where soldiers live, the critical businesses, factories and power plants—all these potential targets have been hardened. Many of these sites are surrounded by huge concrete blast walls that look like Jersey barriers on steroids. Vehicle entrances to all important sites are gated or set up as serpentines, and guarded by well-armed sentries. Inside their camps, soldiers carry their weapons at all times, even when jogging. Mothers who used to warn their sons or daughters against running with scissors would be astonished at the sight of U.S. troops in sneakers, sweating through their daily physical training while holding pistols in their fists.

It has all worked, though. "I just recently returned to Iraq after a few weeks back in Poland," a Baghdad-based official of the Coalition Provisional Authority (CPA) told me in January, "and I was pleasantly surprised to see that security has improved enormously in just the last couple of months. That's great news for everybody. And it really helps my work of getting the economy going again, because a business revival here depends to a great degree on the establishment of basic security."

The so-called Green Zone in central Baghdad, where the most important government offices are located, is essentially a province unto itself. Inside the barriers, all is very quiet—sufficiently so that visitors can strip off their body armor. The building where the CPA and Ambassador Paul Bremer are based is a large former Hussein family palace. Entering the premises requires special passes and a wait—roughly equivalent to visiting the White House. Inside, the headquarters has the slightly sickly air of any bureaucracy (think the Department of Housing and Urban Development, or the Social Security Administration), but in a more garishly opulent setting. The cafeteria is a gossip center for diplomats, journalists, military paper pushers, contractors and hangers-on of all sorts; but during my two visits, very little of substance or interest seemed to be taking place in any of the offices that are crammed, cubicle-style, into former ballrooms and lounges throughout the rambling edifice.

Few U.S. soldiers are injured by attacks on their bases anymore. In many recent months, close to one-quarter of American deaths have been from nonhostile causes like traffic accidents or personal medical conditions. "We had a colonel who shot himself in the foot last week," one officer informed me with a shake of his head and a suppressed grin. "Literally. He was clearing his weapon and not paying attention." The buildings designated as sensitive by the Coalition are now mostly impregnable—which is why the guerillas have taken to attacking markets, local police stations, mosques and other soft targets.

At the anniversary of the Iraq war there were over 200,000 members of various Iraqi security forces—police, facilities guards, Iraq Civil Defense Corps members, and border guards—on duty patrolling their own country. Many of these are ineffective at present. But they will improve. And as it is increasingly the husbands, sons, brothers and fathers of Iraqis themselves who are killed and injured by guerillas, the resistance becomes ever more unpopular.

I ask the soldiers in charge of recruiting and training the Iraqi security forces whether they are having trouble finding recruits (who get paid about $50 a month). They tell me that there are waiting lists of one or two hundred for most every incoming class. And these new security forces are earning the confidence of the Iraqi public. Asked in a five-city November poll commissioned by the State

Department whether local representatives of the Iraqi police are "trusted by most members of the community," 77 percent of Iraqis (including 80 percent of Baghdad residents) said "yes." A February 2004 poll by ABC News found that 68 percent of Iraqis nationwide say thay "have confidence" in their new police; the only group rated higher by the public was "Iraq's religious leaders," who garnered a 70 percent confidence rating.

Most of the freshly minted Iraqi soldiers, guards and police I have observed were very raw; some appeared to be only marginally competent; a few seemed wholly untrustworthy. There have been a few cases of recruits trying to organize anti-American cells within their units, and it's believed that rogue police officers killed some American civilians at a traffic stop in March 2004. In fighting in Fallujah and elsewhere in April, some Iraqi units deserted or flinched badly under fire. But the ranks are gradually being winnowed. Enlistees and officers who prove uncooperative, corrupt or simply cowardly are being let go. While I was in Iraq in early 2004, for instance, two commanders who refused orders to search mosques and execute missions were summarily fired.

One of the factors holding back the Iraqi police and soldiers is a lack of adequate equipment. They begged for radios—in particular, units that would allow them to communicate on the same channels with U.S. forces—nearly every time I saw them interact with their American counterparts. They also need vehicles, and the ICDC need heavier weapons that will allow them to stand up to insurgents attacking with rocket-propelled grenades (RPGs) and machine guns. At present they can only flee from such weaponry.

"What I'm looking for as we work together with the ICDC in the future," states Major General Swannack, "is that we have shared situation awareness. In other words, I can talk on a radio to an ICDC unit, and they can understand what we are doing in concert with what they're doing. We're not there yet. We're still waiting on trucks and radios to fully equip these forces. These are on order and, as I understand it, should be here somewhere in the next sixty to ninety days."

The quality of some Iraqi units is better than others. Colonel Kurt Fuller, commander of the roughly four thousand soldiers from the 82nd in southwestern Baghdad, told me he was confident that he had found a commander for the ICDC unit trained by his men who was selfless, competent and dutiful. "He's a former air defense officer in the Iraqi army—which was probably the most dangerous job in their military while the American Air Force was on the other side—and I think he'll be a very good leader. Our job is to find men like him and put them in charge."

2

THE RECONSTRUCTION BUSINESS

Even as they are preparing to bare their sharp teeth and claws in Operation Tidal Wave, U.S. Army commanders continue to purr at other Baghdadis. For two hours on a Saturday morning, Lieutenant Colonel Dave Haight and his staff of Civil Affairs specialists meet in a building that used to be a city library (albeit lacking any sign of ever having contained books) with the Dawrah Neighborhood Advisory Council—one of the many nascent representative bodies the Army has set up all across Iraq. The nine members of this council (seven of whom are present) represent about one-sixth of Baghdad, or around 450,000 people.

This day they are discussing what public use should be made of a palace compound the 82nd Airborne has just handed over to the council. Previously a residence of Saddam's notorious son Qusay and one of his cousins, the walled property contains half a dozen buildings. The idea that in a public meeting there should be only one conversation at a time seems not to have sunk in yet, but after extensive discussion under the soldiers' guidance, the

35

council decides to devote the largest structure to a women's and children's center. (The Army has been pushing for that choice—here, as elsewhere in Iraq, officers have found that the interests of females are often ignored unless Americans openly protect them.) A second building is slated to become a sports center. Another hall will be the new home of the council itself.

A patient Civil Affairs major named Al Robinson then tells the councilors that the battalion is prepared, on two weeks' notice, to provide $10,000 to furnish the buildings, buy air conditioners and install light fixtures. He explains carefully how this has to be done. The council must draw up a wish list, make a budget, recommend vendors and contractors. At least three alternate suppliers will need to give bids for every purchase—because when spending public money it's important to get the best price possible. There are to be no private dealings or sweetheart arrangements for relatives (a tough concept for Iraqis). Army reservists, called up from civilian jobs ranging from federal marshal to construction supervisor to printer, painstakingly spell out the basics of ethical public management—transparency, honesty, accountability.

It's apparent that some of the members are mulling these notions for the very first time. But there is a quotient of responsible talent in the group. The commander's favorite representative is the sole female, a Baghdad Kurd named Nasreen Hidar Qatar, a doctor who runs a local pediatric clinic. (She is also this sector's representative on the Baghdad City Council, where again she is the only woman.) Other members of the Dawrah Council include a clothing store operator, a retired police officer, a small-business owner, a school administrator (who required a special exemption because he was a Baath Party member) and a retiree.

The council had previously enrolled a tenth member, Majed Abd Musawi, a charismatic natural politician who served as a kind of unofficial leader. Shortly before this meeting, however, the battalion received evidence of petty corruption by Majed. He had channeled money allotted for street sweeping to dead men, children and others in a scheme to enrich himself. He had used a council propane-distribution program to line his own pockets. Now he is in jail awaiting trial. American commanders feel they must be stern in combating the venality that is endemic to Iraqi public life, so in recent months they have made prominent examples of certain grafters.

This tricky effort to plant the seeds of decent governance is managed with extraordinary patience by a small number of soldiers. These excursions deep into the realm of politics and sociology sometimes seem surreal to them. It is chatty, arbitrative work, quite different from the tasks that infantry officers are primarily trained and temperamentally wired for. One of the captains working most closely with the Dawrah Council is an artilleryman. The officer who ended up handling much of the discretionary money that the commander channeled through the council for rebuilding projects last summer was a chemical warfare officer (otherwise underemployed in a guerilla war).

But whatever their private thoughts, all the soldiers taking part in this long morning's discussion are impassive, calm and dogged on the outside. The U.S. Army is focusing hard on reconstructive, civic work of this sort. For officers and soldiers know that in a low-intensity insurgency amidst a civilian population, building up broad local forces of moderation is half the battle.

IMAM TROUBLES

Immediately after the council gathering, the same building hosts another important civic conclave, one with a sharper edge. Commander Haight has been meeting weekly with a circle of neighborhood clerics, and this latest installment could be climactic. Analysis of recorded Friday sermons shows that of the forty-four mosques in Al-Rashid, about nine or ten periodically spout anti-American rhetoric, with four of these inciting actual violence. One of the worst mosques looms just outside the window of the room where the Dawrah Neighborhood Advisory Council meets—a large Sunni mosque known as Mekkad al-Mokaramah, right across the street.

On the previous Wednesday, the imams of the four violence-inciting mosques were individually summoned to the local police station by Haight, presented with evidence of inflammatory rhetoric in their sermons, and informed that if this continued they could suffer serious consequences. Each was required to sign a letter stating that he understood the nature of this "last warning."

I have read transcripts of sermons from nearby mosques. Most avoid political subjects, and many are scrupulously neutral on the fighting in Iraq. A number of them counsel patience and cooperation with the Coalition, rejoicing that "the dark and bad time of Saddam and his people is over now."

But a handful of radical imams, many of them belonging to the Saudi Wahhabi sect, spew vicious, obsessively anti-American, anti-Jewish and anti-Christian rhetoric in sermons that mix prayer with rambling political propagandizing. Here is a sampling of their comments.

Raqueman Mosque:

"In Afghanistan and Bosnia the Americans destroyed everything. You are forbidden to say this is a good year, because it is a Christian year and not a Muslim year." (12/26/03)

"The enemy is in our country. This war is against the Muslim religion. May God kill our enemies." (12/19/03)

"Don't be like the bad people who run to offer Americans help." (12/12/03)

"The enemy wants to exterminate Muslims and start a crusade." (12/5/03)

"Sons of monkeys and pigs came to this country under the name of civilization, technology, and freedom. They mix honey with poison to change our lives. President Bush swears in Congress that he will shave our beards and take the dresses and veils off our women. President Bush swears he will turn every woman into a whore. I ask God to change American conditions from health to sickness. I hope God will finish them, and show them dark days." (11/13/03)

Taheed Mosque:

"God kills the *kaffir* [infidel, a synonym for Americans] and those who support them. God has mercy for and helps the mujahideen [those who attack U.S. forces].

God helps the mujahideen to banish the *kaffir* from our land." (9/25/03)

"Please God, kill the Americans, destroy them, and eject them from Iraq." (9/19/03)

Yasseen Mosque:
"Americans are going to hell. They are unbelievers." (11/28/03)

"Bush is a friend of tyranny and a friend of the devil." (11/21/03)

"The Coalition wants to turn Iraqis into slaves." (9/19/03)

"Bush steals Iraqi money. He is a criminal. Pray to God to finish Bush. God will break the Americans' noses so they cannot see." (9/12/03)

"We will wield our weapons and sacrifice our blood in war against the Jews and Americans." (9/5/03)

Beneath their splendid robes and turbans, most of the imams at this meeting are not impressive. Their complaints are surprisingly trivial and peevish, largely based on rumor, secondhand reports and fear-mongering. Several of the nine Sunni imams howl of alleged threats or incursions from neighborhood Shiites. Saddam coddled the Sunni mosques and persecuted Shiite congregations. The regime change has cheered many of the Shiites and emboldened them to challenge their old Sunni enemies.

The imams also make vague, repetitious and unsubstantiated charges against U.S. soldiers. They cite tendentious Arab TV reports often, personal experience virtually never. There is lots of onerous scapegoating, hardly any productive logic, no offers of useful analysis or practical help.

The American officers on the other side of the table remain amazingly patient as the conversation passes slowly through an Army translator. They proffer thanks. They register factual corrections. They solicit opinions. They calmly refute myths of raped women and defiled sanctuaries. During the course of a year, only two mosques in this densely populated region have been entered by U.S. forces. In one case, a large trove of weapons and explosives was uncovered. In the other, a junior officer forced his way into a mosque where he believed the perpetrators of a mortar attack had fled. They were not found, so Lieutenant Colonel Haight offered private and public apologies and paid for the door that had been broken.

Portions of the two-hour meeting spin into minute politico-religious debate. The imams rail against Jews. The officers explain democracy and religious tolerance. They admit their own shortcomings as military administrators, and bend over backward to be fair and placating. Their diplomacy is what one might expect from politicians rather than from fighting men.

At the end of the day, however, Haight remains blunt and hard-nosed. He informs these religious men that they are free to counsel their flocks and criticize the government however they like, with one exception: they may not encourage violence. Several of the clerics are friendly and conciliatory. Two scowling sheiks, though, both of whom were summoned to the official warning on Wednesday, continue to complain and posture. One—the head of the problem-mosque directly across the street—challenges Haight for the officer's opinion of his recent sermons.

"You want an honest answer? I think you are dangerous, Sheik Akram," replies Haight. "Even after I spoke to you on Wednesday, you broadcast a message on Friday calling for the killing of the enemies of Islam. You know we respect religion, but what you are preaching is not religion, it is criminal activity. I am at the end of my patience." The sheik, claiming translation errors, seems stunned to learn that the remarks in question are preserved in their original on tape. The officer says, "You can come see me if you'd like and I will play you the recording."

Privately Haight tells me, "He has pushed me into an awful position. I am probably going to have to arrest him later this week."

I ask another officer what kind of response could be expected if one of the imams was detained. "Three to five days of neighborhood demonstrations, perhaps some of them rough, but then things would fade. The one thing we can't risk is picking him up only to have him released soon after. That would seem to reward resistance. We have two options: convince Iraq's Religious Ministry to revoke his position at the mosque, or collect enough strong evidence to be certain we can convict him of inciting violence in a legal trial. We've submitted transcripts and are awaiting some decisions now."

The officers involved admit afterward that meetings like this often leave them exhausted; even the most experienced diplomat and talk-marathoner would be challenged to bridge the culture gaps on display in the company of these clerics. For men of action trained in the arts of war, this work can be a reach. They conceal the strain, however, and manage to eke a bit of progress out of what, in less disciplined hands, could have become a useless head-butting contest.

■ ■

Fortunately, Saturday's illustration of Sunni Islam at its most frustrating is not nationally representative. Only about 20 percent of Iraq's population is Sunni, and only a portion of those are under the influence of demagogic clerics who were corrupted by Saddam. The imams who guide Iraq's Shiite majority tend, on the whole, to inspire more confidence.

Sunni leaders are often virtually self-appointed, as Sunnis have no rigorous tradition of theological scholarship or vetting of religious leaders. "The imams I've worked with are unwilling to police themselves," states Colonel Fuller from his Baghdad headquarters. "We've asked them to hold each other accountable and to sanction their own radicals, but they do nothing." Shiite clergy, on the other hand, rise through a system of tutelage and hierarchy, which often weeds out extremists and self-seekers. They must pursue exacting study for years to reach high-ranking positions. As a result, fewer are rabble-rousers and many are genuine intellectuals.

I ask Captain Ken Burgess, a company commander who worked extensively with local imams during the early months when the Coalition was scrambling to find Iraqi leaders outside the existing regime, whether he saw differences in quality between Shiite and Sunni sheiks.

"Absolutely," he answers immediately. "In my experience, the Shia are more influenced by facts, more rational, more responsive to evidence we might present. They are also more worldly, better educated, less small-minded. They seem less susceptible to the urban myths and superstitions we are often battling with the Sunni clerics, and they are definitely less likely to practice the petty slander and libel against others that is so characteristic of the Sunni sheiks."

In a nation where Shiites are the large majority, this provides reason to hope that Iraq might eventually develop a more responsible religious politics.

CORDON AND SEARCH

On Sunday morning, the focus at 2nd Battalion shifts sharply from diplomacy back to military counterinsurgency. In the predawn dark and chill, I pile into the back of a cargo Humvee with ten paratroopers as Operation Tidal Wave kicks off. These soldiers have been charging across Iraq, out on operations nearly every day, for almost a full year, and their clothes show it. The crisp new desert-camouflage uniforms I remember from when I was with them in early 2003 are now stained and frayed. Helmet covers and gloves are threadbare. Even Colonel Fuller wears a cap as creased and begrimed as a coal miner's Levis. These are veteran, combat-hardened soldiers. They can carry out an arrest or clear a room in a blink. Their fighting instincts are automatic.

Every time these men venture onto the roads, there is tension. They know the risks. In my first five days in

Baghdad, five IEDs detonated and five more were uncovered and defused. In addition, there have been fifteen assaults on Coalition forces with rockets, grenades, mortars or small arms—most of them ineffective.

Last night, just before we went to bed, we got word of yet another IED attack, this time on the main road outside the brigade's southwest Baghdad headquarters. Fortunately the explosion went off between two Humvees, directly hitting neither. The armored windshield of one vehicle was smashed, but no one was hurt.

On this moonlit night we snake into a sector not far from downtown that is nonetheless quite rural and isolated—thanks to the abysmal roads, thick riverside vegetation, and tribal clannishness that keeps residents closed off by themselves. This is a dangerous area, where numerous recent attacks, including the double murder of January 2, have occurred. A long string of high-mobility trucks slithers down mucky country lanes bordered by tall vertical-thatch fences and rude mud-walled huts. There is a strong smell of animal dung. Dogs yap from their sleep. A rooster crows.

Suddenly the sky lights up as attack helicopters hit the three sites of recent assaults. F-15s thunder low overhead. All morning long they will circle and screech, serving chiefly as psychological weapons.

The paratroopers pour out of their trucks, spread themselves in lines across neglected fields where straggly weeds have sprouted after the winter rains, and begin to walk north. Each time a farmhouse is encountered, a squad of soldiers circle it, bang on the door or gate, then enter and search for weapons. Each household is allowed one AK-47 and one magazine of rounds; anything more is confiscated. Some suspicious pamphlets and tattered old military publications are examined and handed to translators—are they Baath propaganda or training manuals?

I am patrolling with the roughly twenty-five remaining members of 3rd Platoon of Bravo Company. This is the unit Seiden and Bangayan belonged to until their deaths a week and a half earlier. The men are controlled and well behaved. There were some angry flashes the night before as they discussed going into the place where their buddies had been slain, but this morning they are cool and professional. There is no roughness to the searching. They are solicitous to families and unemotional with the men. They offer Arabic salutations to the women as they leave.

The domiciles are squalid—dingy mud and slapdash concrete structures containing no furniture and almost no food. There are few possessions of any sort beyond a handful of cows, donkeys and geese in each farmyard and an occasional rattletrap vehicle. Running water is nonexistent and sewer seepage trickles through yards consistently littered with trash. Family members of all ages sleep in a single room on thin cloths stretched across the ground.

These are not people who benefited from the previous regime. It is hard to know what motivates any of them to resist the chance for a new Iraq other than intense, reactionary ignorance, perhaps religious fanaticism, and quite possibly cash payments from insurgency organizers. All over the Sunni Triangle, insurgent cells have been paying poor Iraqis hundreds or even thousands of dollars to plant and detonate roadside bombs or shoot rocket-propelled grenades at security forces.

This region has been trouble from the beginning. Back in October, the soldiers conducting this morning's search uncovered the largest ammunition cache found in Baghdad—a huge stash buried on the grounds of a mosque bordering the Tigris, which included 2,000 rockets, 357 landmines, 207 artillery shells, and cases and cases of small-arms ammunition, anti-aircraft rounds and fuses. The 2nd Battalion's engineers removed some of the ordnance and destroyed the rest in place; there was a series of spectacular explosions that took all day and left excavations that literally rerouted the Tigris.

As the troopers proceed from house to house, they round up all the adult males, creating a long file of dark, staring eyes. Near the river, various platoons herd the men into several large groups. Military intelligence officers begin to collect their names and to photograph groupings of brothers, fathers and sons, and cousins. The digital images will be stored on their laptops for future reference. After many months of operating in the area, these soldiers know the family networks surprisingly well. Several men are pulled out for questioning: two wanted siblings, a one-eyed old coot known to be the caretaker of Sheik Thoma's mosque, the father of a man whom farmers saw digging along the road just before the January 2 bombing.

Then the PsyOps Humvees topped with big speakers pull up and broadcast a message from brigade commander Fuller:

Attention men of Karb Degla!
Ten days ago, there was an attack on a Coalition patrol near here. This attack, and other attacks throughout the

country, slow progress, hurt innocent Iraqis, and delay the withdrawal of Coalition forces from Iraq.

This is your notice. We hold you responsible for the security situation in your area. Provide us with information on those who continue their futile attacks. Help us rid your community of these cancers.

Do not confuse our restraint today with weakness. You know our capability, and you know we can and will direct it against our enemies. Today we came as concerned friends; do not make us come back as enemies.

WALKING A TIGHTROPE

Shortly after receiving this warning, reinforced by leaflets given to each detainee, the frozen-faced men of Karb Degla are sent home. Lieutenant Colonel Haight drives me a few hundred meters up the road to the site of the January 2 blast. The crater is six feet deep. On the other side of the road there are blood stains and crushed vegetation where the smashed Humvee careened down an embankment. "Those men were so perforated by shrapnel we had to lift their bodies out on ponchos," says the colonel grimly. "This was a bad, bad day I don't want repeated."

Neither does Lieutenant Andrew Blickhahn, who commands the 3rd Platoon. He was in the lead vehicle of the two-truck patrol when the bomb detonated, and he ran back to organize return fire and rescue of the survivors. An enlisted soldier who later attended West Point and became an officer, Blickhahn is a cool, quiet character who shows no sign of being shaken by the fact that he has been attacked in three close calls since arriving in Baghdad—twice by IEDs and once in a mortar ambush.

Around noon the lieutenant is asked to take his platoon to the nearby Baghdad sewer plant. The father of the man spotted digging on the road shortly before the bombing has been handed over to his men by the military intelligence officers managing the morning roundup. The old man states that his son—Mohammed Ahmed Jassim—works at the plant. In a state of advanced decay when the Coalition arrived, the treatment plant is currently undergoing a massive reconstruction managed by the Bechtel Corporation. Hundreds of laborers swarm the sprawling grounds—shoveling, pushing wheelbarrows, troweling concrete.

About twenty paratroopers in three trucks pull up at the plant. It occurs to me that this is a classic instance of the way American officers are required to mix hard and soft tactics. On the one hand, the man who murdered two members of this platoon may be right there under their noses; military considerations alone would call for charging in hard, seizing employment rosters and racing to grab him. But this plant is more than just Jassim's workplace; it is also one of the most important projects in the rebuilding of Baghdad—a major source of local jobs and income, a critical element in improving the quality of life in the city, a centerpiece of the reconstruction effort. Inflaming the Iraqi technocrats managing the project could damage the "soft" side of the counterinsurgency effort, whereas cultivating them could lead, down the road, to valuable cooperation from a critical civic institution.

Lieutenant Blickhahn walks the tightrope between military objectives and social rebuilding. In the end, he takes a diplomatic, unaggressive approach. Several sites are searched. All managers swear they know of no Mohammed Jassim. There is no way to tell if they are being honest. The patrol finally leaves empty-handed.

But they send home a note with Jassim's father: "Coalition forces want to speak with you. Report immediately to the authorities nearest you. We know where you live."

■ ■

Civic reconstruction as a tactic of counterinsurgency is not something foreign to the Army. Major Mark Stock, the 2nd Battalion's efficient executive officer, is a fair-haired, thick-limbed, barrel-chested West Point graduate and unquestionably first and foremost a military man, but he also holds a master's degree in public administration from Harvard's Kennedy School of Government. In Iraq, Stock often has occasion to exercise his administrative skills. He helped orchestrate Iraqi contractors to quickly set up concrete barracks where hundreds of men could live and work—"for less than what it would cost to build a good single-family house in the part of New York state my wife comes from," he notes with a smile.

Stock and other officers also helped organize a lightning effort to improvise armor for the battalion's Humvees. Airborne vehicles are designed to be light so they can be parachuted out of planes. But when the roadside-bomb threat burst onto the scene at the end of the summer, the thin fiberglass and canvas body panels of their vehicles left the 82nd's soldiers utterly without protection.

It happens that one of the sites guarded by the division is home to Baghdad's petroleum refinery as well as its steel plant. Because these are crucial industrial complexes and workplaces for thousands of men, 120 or so troopers from Bravo Company were stationed early last summer to live in their midst. By their mere armed daily presence they provide security around the clock.

So it was easy for the 82nd's officers to strike up a collaboration with the steel-plant managers on making protective plates for the Humvees. Through trial and error and some live-fire tests that the soldiers enjoyed conducting, the American paratroopers and Iraqi metal fabricators came up with practical homemade designs for new Humvee doors, floor and roof reinforcements, and truck bedliners made from heavy sheets of rolled steel. During October, the battalion's officers got the rough-and-ready designs installed on their entire vehicle fleet for $24,800. These succeeded so well that the rest of the Army units in Baghdad soon contracted with the plant to manufacture the impromptu armor for their vehicles as well. The Army's whole transport fleet now looks like something from *The Beverly Hillbillies*, but the soldiers feel a lot safer.

FIXER FIGHTERS

Flexibility and inventive problem solving are a critical part of battlefield operations, and the 82nd is especially good at these. Particularly early on, when there were many pressing demands on the occupying forces, few rules, and no bureaucracy in Iraq, soldiers freelanced their way over thousands of obstacles. There was a premium on getting the job done, and one of the reasons they were able to move so fast is because operations were highly decentralized.

Major Pete Wilhelm, the director of day-to-day battle operations for the 2nd Battalion, reports that there were "lots of times when a company commander under me would get time-sensitive information, act on it, take casualties, and evacuate his casualties before I even heard about it. That's just the way we've had to operate."

This same pattern also held true on the civil-reconstruction side. Officers used CERP (the Commanders' Emergency Response Program) as an almost instantaneous tool for jumpstarting Iraqi society. Employing dollars that had been seized from the old regime, the effort channeled discretionary money to battalion commanders in $250,000 chunks, leaving them remarkably free to allot it according to their best judgment. In small $200-$10,000 payments, these funds have been used to rehabilitate thousands of schools, to pick up garbage and connect sewer and water lines, to hire security guards and police for critical sites, to provision the meeting rooms of the new neighborhood councils.

I repeatedly ask officers I meet whether it isn't perhaps asking too much to expect the same warriors who fought their way into Iraq to then do much of the political and sociological work of putting the country back together. Many surprise me by saying it hasn't been an undue strain, and that the task of civil reconstruction is often closely linked to military responsibilities.

Ken Burgess is a stocky, pug-nosed company commander who was heavily involved in the Army's early-summer efforts to set up the first advisory councils in every district

of Baghdad. "When we first arrived we didn't know anything about the neighborhoods—not even the street names
and physical boundaries, much less the disposition of the
people living there. Just to be able to operate militarily, we
desperately needed mechanisms where residents could talk
to us and give us a pulse on what people were thinking.

"In the beginning it was tremendously subjective.
Some people came to us and volunteered to help. Many
we just grabbed. Any time I ran into an Iraqi who struck
me as a potential leader, I would start a conversation with
an eye to deciding whether that person might be a good
neighborhood representative. I often had to rely on my
gut instincts, and of course I wasn't always right.

"But soldiers actually tend to be pretty skilled at this
kind of work. A huge fraction of military officers were captains of their soccer teams, scout leaders, student government officers, whatever. They understand leadership. Even
at the enlisted level, the basic essence of being a good sergeant is to be a quick study of character, a master of motivation, a strong communicator, someone who really
understands human nature. A lot of basic military work
is inherently 'sociological,' and this has helped us in our
crash effort to building up a working society here.

"Yes, there are times when one of your soldiers gets
killed in a military operation, and it becomes incredibly
hard to go out the next day and shake hands and wave
to the kids. That's a normal emotional thing. But the skills
needed for 'nation building' are already right there in
many officers."

Still, it's not easy. Colonel Kurt Fuller, as brigade commander, has been the martial sovereign of 1.6 million

people in southwestern Baghdad over the last year. He's a grizzled, scarred, drawling Oklahoma native, and very much a straight shooter. When I press him on the extraordinary demands he and his men have faced in carrying out political and civic reconstruction, he answers: "I have been frustrated by the lengths we've had to go on this. My mission statement says I'm responsible for creating a safe and secure environment so that the Coalition Provisional Authority and the Iraqis themselves can establish a government. I'm not trained as a diplomat, as an administrator. Yet when I go to the neighborhood meetings the CPA chairs are often empty.

"I need their advice, but I've not gotten it. The governance piece, especially, I am uncomfortable with, as are all of my commanders. Hell, I'd never even sat in on a city council meeting back home before I came here. We've had to set an awful lot in motion without much help.

"On the other hand, we're probably the only ones who can do this. We've got the manpower, the resources. We're out there on the streets. So I've just tried to apply common sense. And I guess the bottom line is that it has mostly worked. Judged in any historical sense, we're approaching a wildly successful end result. In a difficult urban environment, amidst a guerilla insurgency, we're getting a broken society working again. So I suppose that's all that matters."

■ ■

It seems something of an irony that the U.S. Army—traditionally known as mean but hardly lean when it comes to bureaucracy—has turned out to be the fast-moving, practical, reliable, red-tape-free alternative in Iraq. The civilian Coalition Provisional Authority, the U.S. Agency for International Development and the State Department have done lots of paper-shuffling on Iraq. But these haven't contributed even a tiny fraction of the critical grunt work the Army has carried out to repair this society.

Meanwhile, the international charities, U.N.-related agencies and "nongovernmental organizations" that profess to specialize in social reconstruction have been almost wholly absent from the field—in part because of a scandalous politicization that has made them chary of "underwriting an American occupation," as tendentious spokesmen even from major organizations like the International Red Cross put it. Some do-good organizations have actually gone beyond unhelpfulness into active obstruction. Iraqi papers reported in January that a number of "peace, anti-imperialist and anti-globalization organizations" in Europe have actually launched a campaign to send financial contributions to "resisters" committing attacks against the Coalition forces and their projects in Iraq.

So the interesting reality is this: it is primarily to armed U.S. warfighters that everyday Iraqis—lacerated by years of war, governmental neglect and international indifference—owe the hard-won progress in making their communities more humane. The Iraqis understand this. It's not clear whether the American public does.

3

DEMOCRACY SCHOOL

In Iraq, the roles of good cop and bad cop must be filled by the same American soldiers, and today it's time for the 82nd to rap some knuckles. Two of the most inflammatory imams in southern Baghdad—Sheik Akram of the Mekkad al-Mokaramah mosque, and Sheik Riyad of Abu Bakr—have been summoned to appear before Colonel Fuller. Despite having been called to the police station on Wednesday and read the riot act by Lieutenant Colonel Haight, both imams repeated thinly veiled threats against Coalition forces in their latest Friday sermons. Something has got to give.

The U.S. commanders don't know exactly where the imams live and—though Iraqi police have been dispatched to each mosque with a summons—aren't sure they will show up for today's meeting. Finally, perhaps a half-hour late, a car pulls up. The two sheiks mill about for a while with their entourages, then walk over to greet Fuller and Haight where they wait outside the appointed building. Sheik Akram wears a kind of dished turban on his head and a floor-length cream tunic. Over two long meetings where I have had a chance to observe him, Akram has struck me as deceptive, although a bit simple. His eyes shift rapidly and he often shrugs his shoulders and cracks a pained satirical smile. Sheik Riyad, chubby, dark-bearded and wearing a white shawl over his head and shoulders that always holds an exquisite little crease where it falls above his nose, is brighter but even less transparent; he is openly haughty, arrogant and dripping with disdain.

Once again, the American commanders exhibit bottomless patience—if anything, erring on the side of being too enduring, in my judgment. They earnestly lay out American concepts of faith, toleration and free speech. Colonel Fuller has studied the Qur'an this summer, and he asks the two clerics to explain their understanding of what the book teaches on religious belief, Godliness, jihad, and killing. He asks them to be specific about who are "the enemies of Islam" (which they refer to ritually in their sermons). The conversation snakes its way through an Army interpreter, somewhat painfully, over a period of two and a half hours.

Fuller allows Sheik Riyad a long speech on the American deficiencies that create armed resistance in Iraq. Point three on the sheik's six-point list is that during nighttime raids, women may be seen in their nightdresses. And men may be treated roughly. He offers no examples of abuse, but seems certain that these are standard U.S. Army infractions. By this time I have observed about two dozen house searches and accompanied troopers on three dead-of-night arrests; I have seen no hint of such untoward behavior.

In one of these raids, led by an Arabic-speaking U.S. Special Forces soldier, a suspected ex-Fedayeen arms dealer was picked up. A team of twenty soldiers drove up to the house in full blackout, surrounded the entrances, jumped the gate, used a ram to pop the front door, then cleared the building room by room. All women and children were gently segregated into one location. The men were interrogated by an Iraqi translator (his face obscured by a balaclava), and the wanted party was identified. Rooms were quickly and unobtrusively searched for weapons. Then the detainee was taken away for further questioning, and remaining family members were left unbothered.

The second raid, seeking a security guard who had offered some fellow guards a chance to make extra money by transporting explosives to Fallujah, was virtually identical, except that instead of battering the front door (something that is done only where violence is feared), the troopers knocked. (Had there been no response, or had they been fired upon or been refused access, they would have forced entry.) The third raid, seeking an informer who had failed to identify some insurgents as promised, was also a knock-and-go.

In the following weeks, I would observe many more raids, interrogations, searches and other police actions. All were carried out professionally and with respect for personal dignity and property. Whenever it was necessary to interact with an Iraqi woman, great deference was shown; I witnessed no female searches, but was told that when deemed necessary they are done solely by female soldiers. I observed that children were always treated with kindness, and often affection, by U.S. soldiers.

READING THE RIOT ACT

After hearing out Sheik Riyad, and explaining the rules under which raids are conducted, Colonel Fuller gets to the heart of the matter. "While we go to great lengths to be respectful, and avoid embarrassing people, you must understand that our actions are often a matter of life and death. I am responsible for stopping terrorists who have killed and hurt hundreds of people in this area. And I need the help of all good people in the community.

"Unfortunately we know that there are imams who support terrorists, and who actually encourage terrorist attacks. In fact, many of the terrorists we see act on religious grounds. You must know that the freedom of speech carries with it great responsibilities. In particular, you cannot incite violence. A real holy man would never do that anyway.

"So I need to know today whether you two are my allies or my enemies. I suppose you will both say you are not my enemy, as you have in the past. But then in your public statements to your followers you call for death to the enemies of Islam, and violent opposition to occupiers, and so forth. What am I to do?"

Akram recognizes that this is a climactic conversation, and finally answers carefully: "Iraq is our country, but it is now occupied. We must accept the status quo. So I am going to try to avoid these subjects that have created misunderstanding."

Haight confronts him forcefully: "But you told me that on Wednesday. And then you went right out on Friday and conjured up more violence anyway. You know what? You may deny you are instigating attacks, but when you say people should attack 'infidels' and 'the enemies of Islam,' they think of one thing: this uniform [tugging hard at his own sleeve]. And you both know that!"

Akram: "In my Friday prayers I asked God to 'kill the enemies of religion, wherever you find them, split them, destroy them, wherever you find them.' I did not say Americans or British."

Fuller, exploding: "I don't care who you said to kill! You cannot tell people to kill others. No holy man would do that! Where does the Qur'an sanction such a thing?"

Akram: "I have been doing that for twenty years. Saddam never objected to this."

Haight: "Then you've been wrong for twenty years."

Akram: "OK. I'm not going to say it from now on."

Fuller: "Yeah, and you promised that last time, then broke your word just a few days later."

Akram: "When you asked me to this meeting, I consulted with my mentor at the Religious Science Organization. He counseled me to avoid words like 'enemies,' 'unbelievers' and so forth, so I am going to try. I will preach only about patience, the Qur'an and such. I will leave the problem alone now."

Dodging, rationalizing and backpedaling when forced to, Akram and Riyad are skating at the brink of arrest for inciting violence. But American officers throughout Iraq are striving mightily to avoid such detainments. They go out of their way to show respect for imams, mosques and the Muslim religion so as not to feed paranoia that the U.S. presence in Iraq is part of a crusade against Islam.

They also know, as a practical matter, that such arrests can lead to civil disorder. When they arrested one renegade sheik in 2003, a thousand of his followers blocked the main highway through that part of Baghdad, making news all around the globe. "We knew we were knocking down a hornets' nest but couldn't accept his behavior any longer, so we arrested him," reports Fuller. In a well-organized show of American force, the road was eventually cleared by five companies of soldiers, who flex-cuffed the ringleaders of the blockade and trucked them away.

Colonel Fuller later told me he thought he would have no alternative but to arrest the two sheiks at this meeting. In the end, though, he issues another stern warning and sends them home. Whether these men are active partisans of the resistance or just religious fanatics too zealous to care about the effects of their words on their congregations is not clear. Also unclear is whether they realize how close they are to being locked away and charged. But they will get no more free passes.

"That's it," says the colonel to his officers after they leave. "If those men cross the line again, you roll them up."

SHEIKDOWN

Within one five-hour period this January afternoon I watched the sun go down on the old Iraq and begin to rise on a new and very different nation. The old Iraq arrived in the person of a conclave of Sunni sheiks. "Sheik" is an honorific term (roughly, "chief") that is applied to

Muslim clerics, but is also used to designate the secular leaders who head Iraq's tribes—the blood-based, extended-family clans that used to be the main centers of authority in the country, and that still survive as quasi-political, quasi-social, quasi-economic power blocs.

The Sunni tribal leaders, who had real influence under Saddam Hussein, in many places have refused to meet with Coalition forces, and have mostly failed to cooperate with the new institutions being set up across the nation by Americans. Very likely, many of the men I am studying across a large boardroom-style table as I type this have been involved in fomenting the resistance in Iraq. But today, a few weeks after Saddam's arrest, Dave Elsen, the young captain who serves as military intelligence officer of 3rd Battalion of the 325th Regiment, has orchestrated something of a breakthrough. Working with Dr. Arshad Ali Mohammed, a professor of Arabic literature at Mustanseriyah University and chairman of the Al-Rashid District Advisory Council, whom Elsen has come to like and trust through their mutual work on neighborhood councils, a meeting has been arranged between American officers and an association of Sunni sheiks from around the country. Arshad is himself a Shiite, but a man respected by Iraqis of many stripes.

The meeting takes place at the Hunt Club—a notorious social hangout of Qusay Hussein that has recently been converted into headquarters for the Al-Rashid Council. The hunting reference points to falconry, but there's little sign of that noble diversion here. The main distinguishing features of the club are a crude hot tub, a barbeque pit and two traditional Iraqi bread-baking ovens located behind the rather gaudy main building, which looks like a disco hall.

These days, the main bases for the tribal sheiks are poor farm villages, and this group does not display much learning or sophistication. The primary impression the members give is of demagogic, string-pulling fixers and influence merchants. They open the meeting with gripes that there are too few Sunnis on the democracy councils around the country, which is true—but only because most Sunnis refused to participate when the councils were set up.

One particularly corpulent and oleaginous bossman reminisces fondly about Saddam Hussein for a minute, cluelessly representing him as a model: "Many times Saddam did us favors, and many times we did him favors. We worked closely together. Not like today, where nobody offers us the respect we deserve. We must have 'weight' in society. You make us lose face with our people."

Another sheik baldly proposes payola. "We should have a quota, a certain cut," he says through the Army translator. "You give Sheik So-and-So this many jobs. A different sheik gets another group of positions. We need many things: cars, phones, weapons permits."

These men don't get it.

When the company commanders and Civil Affairs officers of the U.S. Army first started seeking out Iraqi leaders during the summer of 2003, they reached out to the tribal leaders as an obvious starting point. Very soon, though, they were put off by the ignorance of the sheiks, their clawing scrappiness and badmouthing of each other, their inflated claims of importance and jealous influencemongering. By the end of the summer, most of the sheiks had been dropped as serious players.

A thin, quick-witted Iraqi who advises the Coalition Provisional Authority has impressed me with his remarks at a couple of meetings. Now he leans over to me and whispers: "Iraqi tribals—they want to make a *deal*. They won't help you out on anything unless you *give* them something." He rolls his eyes on his way out of the room.

SEEDS OF DEMOCRACY

Saddamism amounted to little more than this sort of corrupt, bullying tribal politics, with a heavy dollop of pathological violence added on top. That was the old Iraq: simply the remnant of a premodern, logrolling style of authoritarianism.

The new Iraq, at least as it is sought by the best of a fresh group of Iraqis now taking up roles in the advisory councils, is very different. Dr. Arshad and Dr. Nasreen— intelligent, soft-spoken coalition builders who listen well, assist avidly, but don't trade in favors—embody the ideals of a possible new era in Iraqi politics. The vice chairman of the Al-Rashid District Advisory Council under Dr. Arshad is Khadija Rissan Nama, an agricultural engineer and a woman. In the beginning, U.S. commanders had to push hard to get women on the councils at all, but this fall her fellow councilors actually elected Ms. Khadija into the No. 2 spot on this body, which represents 1.6 million people.

Other members of the Al-Rashid Council include a driver, a radiologist, a lawyer, a phone operator, a veterinarian, an ayatollah, a shopkeeper, a student. Many of them work under death threats; some have been physically attacked. In September, Dr. Akila al-Hashimi, a member of the national Iraqi Governing Council who lived in Al-Rashid, was assassinated as she stepped out of her home.

At today's meeting, a colonel from the newly organized Iraqi police talks about security issues. He is a career police officer who has earned the trust of American commanders. The discussion centers around ways to improve the public image and legitimacy of the Iraqi police and to reduce crime in the city. The street crime rate here is not nearly so bad as media reports would have you believe, however. American Enterprise Institute scholar John Lott calculated in late December 2003 that, despite the war-related disruptions and the fact that Saddam released all of Iraq's common criminals a few days before Americans entered his country, the murder rate in Baghdad is now lower than in most major cities of Europe and America.

Though this advisory council was appointed, not elected, a good deal of thought has gone into a system that continually refines the representative nature of this body and others like it, gradually edging the country toward full democracy. Just in the half-year since its establishment, this council has been "refreshed" twice: the Army has established a mechanism that periodically pushes four individuals off the council by a vote of the members. This gives the councilors a chance to purge corrupt or obstructionist peers. And it provides the community with a regular opportunity to inject new blood into the body. A town hall forum is held (four hundred people came to the last one in Bayaa), and the citizens present elect replacements for the removed members. This represents the dawn of democratic process in Baghdad.

This process allows some openings for extremist candidates, if they can pack the town hall with their supporters. But so far, most of the individuals brought in this way have been responsible. And even the radicals are probably less threatening inside the system, Army officers reason, than they would be agitating from without.

Among the thirty-two members of the Al-Rashid Council (representing about a quarter of Baghdad), there are, however, just three or four Sunnis. In a city where they make up the largest single chunk of the population, this is a problem. But it is a problem created by uncooperative Sunnis themselves, and its solution rests mostly on their own shoulders. Some form of a dramatically different Iraq is coming; the only question is whether the Sunnis will participate in defining it.

THE SELF-RULE REVOLUTION

Some critics of the Iraq war suggest that the whole idea of initiating representative government in the Muslim Middle East is pie in the sky. Certainly there is good reason to be careful about trying to remake the whole world in our democratic image—a task that could keep America busy to the point of exhaustion over several lifetimes. But neither is there any reason for us to be lazy and timid in thinking that today's bullies and strongmen must always hold power.

In the early 1970s, when I first began to read newspapers and follow public life seriously, there was a grand total of forty democratic societies across the globe. Democracy, it was said, simply wouldn't grow in certain kinds of soil. But then stony lands like Portugal, Spain, Greece, Korea, Taiwan, the Philippines, Indonesia, nearly all of Latin America, all of Eastern Europe, and South Africa began to hold free elections for the first time ever. Many of these dramatic turnovers took place in a blink. Today, just thirty years later, there are 120 democracies, 30 of these being nations where civilian rule replaced a military government. The fraction of the world's nations electing their own rulers has increased from one third to two thirds.

There is nothing absurd about the idea that the Arab lands should be next in this development. In fact, there are many good reasons to press energetically in that direction. People who argue that Islam is irreconcilably at odds with democracy forget that half the world's Muslims already live in basic democracies, in countries like Turkey, Indonesia, India, Pakistan and Bangladesh. The main chokepoint for self-rule has been one specific part of the Islamic world—the twenty-one Arab nations. Lebanon was a democracy for more than two decades between World War II and the 1970s; other than that, Arabia has been a desert for representative government.

Iraq is probably the very best place in the Arab world to start changing this. For one thing, the previous government was as abominable as any on the globe. And Iraq is capable of much better. Long the center of learning for the Arab world, present-day Mesopotamia has 22 universities and 43 technical institutes and colleges. And the five million Iraqis living abroad, most of them educated professionals and businesspeople in successful countries, represent another source of experience with modernity that the nation can draw upon as it seeks to lead other Arabs away from autocracy.

Our media regularly inform Americans that extremists from all over the Middle East now view Iraq as the place to dig in their heels and resist liberalizing reforms. What we hear less often is that there are also millions of Middle Easterners disgusted by the self-immolating failures of their nations over the last generation, who now look toward Iraq with hope. One such person, in fact, is a forty-five-year-old cleric named Ayatollah Khomeini. He is the grandson of the Ayatollah Khomeini who unseated the shah of Iran and inaugurated the Middle Eastern tradition of sticking needles in Uncle Sam's eyes back in the late 1970s. Like his grandfather, this ayatollah is a devout Shiite cleric. But that's where the resemblance ends. His grandfather's brand of Islamic theocracy has been an abject failure, he told a Washington, D.C., crowd at the American Enterprise Institute this winter, which is why he has taken up residence in Iraq (in the city of Karbala) to study that country's route to reform. He hopes to encourage the "liberation" of his native Iran as the next project of supporters of reason, liberty and peace in the Middle East.

THE UPSIDE OF IRAQ'S DIVISIONS

Another stumbling block in the way of Iraqi self-rule, critics often claim, is the fact that the nation is divided among three very different ethno-religious groups of roughly equivalent influence. How can the Kurds in the north, the Sunnis in the middle of the country, and the Shiites in the south act as one nation? It's true that there are many different points of view represented among the disparate factions in Iraq. Journalist Amir Taheri has sketched out a few of the main splits:

> The Arab Sunnis want Iraq described as "part of the Arab nation." This is opposed by the Kurds, who say the constitution must describe Iraq as a "bi-national: Arab and Kurdish" state. The Shiites, some 60 percent of the population, reject both the Arab and the "bi-national" formulae. Instead, they wish to emphasize the concept of Iraqiness.
>
> The Kurds want Iraq to become a federal state so that they can enjoy autonomy in their provinces. This is opposed by Arab Sunnis and Shiites who want a centralized state to control the oil revenue and organize the use of water resources.
>
> Some parties, both Sunni and Shiite, want Islam acknowledged as the religion of the state in the new constitution. Other parties oppose this; they want a secular system.
>
> Some parties want Iraq to withdraw from OPEC, the Arab League, and the Organization of the Islamic Conference, and, instead, seek some form of association with the European Union. Others insist that the new constitution should preserve Iraq's traditional foreign relations.
>
> Several parties and personalities want a clause for peace and cooperation with all nations to be included in the constitution. They see this as a step towards an eventual recognition of Israel. Others, however, insist

that Iraq should not recognize Israel until there is a solution to the Palestinian problem.

There are deep divisions on economic philosophy. The Kurds, and some Arab Sunnis, seek a welfare state in which the public sector provides the basic services free of charge. Many Shiites want a free-enterprise market economy to prepare Iraq for joining the World Trade Organization.

There are divisions on the electoral system. The Kurds and Sunni Arabs want proportional representations, with measures that could prevent Shiites from using simple majority rule to impose their will. The Shiites want a first-past-the-post system.

Sounds like a mess, doesn't it? Well, not really. Rather, it sounds like the jousting that breaks out wherever democratic politics is tolerated.

American journalists, who thrive on friction, have focused particularly on religious radicals in their reporting from Iraq over the last year. One favorite, dramatic, precooked storyline is to profile Restive Muslim Zealots on the March Against America! And you can certainly find them in Iraq.

But there are also many other, very different movements rippling through Iraq today that we hear little or nothing of. On December 10, 2003, for instance, twenty thousand Baghdadis marched across the city shouting: "No, no to terrorism! Yes, yes to democracy!" Labor groups sang out in Arabic: "We need factories, we need peace, no fascists, no radicals." Western television hardly mentioned the event, but one of the march leaders declared live on al-Jazeera television, "We will not allow the remnant of the intelligence service of Saddam to destroy this new experiment of democracy and freedom."

Just as many media commentators have emphasized the worst aspects of Iraq's internal splits, they have also sometimes exaggerated the dangers of external pressures on Iraq. It's true that the Iranians encourage Iraq's Shiites, and that the Saudis do the opposite, trying to build up Sunni Wahhabis. It's true that Syria would like to protect the Baathists who used to run the country, and that Kurds from several nations are bolstering their cousins in northern Iraq who hate the Baathists. The Turks, meanwhile, are working to keep the Kurds on a leash. Once again, a picture of fractured chaos, right?

I don't think so. The fact that Iraq's neighbors are working at cross purposes may not be a bad thing at all; it's certainly preferable to the situation we faced in Vietnam, for instance, where most of the neighbors were united behind one faction—the communists.

Likewise, let me suggest that the existence of many poles of influence *inside* Iraq may be a very good thing. The fact that Iraq's Shiites, Sunnis and Kurds are all important, all influential, and not aligned in the same direction may be the single best guarantor of true consensual governance in Iraq. Because none of the three major ethnic/religious blocs will be able to dominate the others, they are going to have to work together, compromise on big questions and respect minority rights. Unlike more homogeneous nations like Iran or Saudi Arabia, Iraqis will never swing wildly together and all go off the deep end at the same time.

With no one able to wield a whip hand, the various factions will serve as checks and balances on each other, in classic democratic fashion. As much as certain Shiite imams might desire a monolithic Islamic government, they will get nowhere without respecting the provincial autonomy that the Kurds demand. If some Sunnis imagine a Baath Party revival might be possible down the road, the Shiites in the south will give them a very rude awakening. Iraqis who want a socialized economy will not be able to run roughshod over the majority who prefer free markets. And so forth.

I don't mean to minimize the tricky negotiations that will be necessary to reconcile these divisions. But this is a prescription for rough-and-tumble democratic horse-trading—not for totalitarianism. With U.S. soldiers present to make sure the disagreements don't flame into armed conflict, I suspect that Iraq's very complexity is likely (after lots of fumbling and toe-stubbing) to result in a surprisingly balanced set of national rules governing the division of political power, religious rights, economic freedom, ethnic protections and regional autonomy. Not because Iraqis are sweet people, but because no one faction is going to be able to dominate the others.

That was the country's experience in March 2004 when it came time to hammer out an interim constitution. Each of the factions that Amir Taheri sketches above had to make plenty of compromises on their wish list. And after tough negotiations, the many viewpoints represented on Iraq's national Governing Council approved a truly remarkable document. Iraq's very first consensual constitution includes a broad bill of rights and wide protections for minorities. Extremist demands that Islamic *sharia* be enshrined as the law of the land were rejected. There is a federalist structure that allows sub-regions considerable latitude to experiment with differing economic, cultural and political solutions.

In sum, Iraq's interim constitution is an amazingly benign charter, encapsulating ideals of individual liberty and due process that have never previously gotten even a toehold in an Arab nation. While this draft will surely evolve once there is an elected government in place to revisit these subjects, the document is a historic accomplishment that will strongly affect the future basis of government not only in Iraq but across the Middle East.

And this feat emerged from the very fractures and diversity of interests that many Iraq pessimists bemoan. Perhaps more outsiders will soon begin to see the point I have long been arguing: that ethnic and religious heterogeneity in Iraq can also work to our advantage, by canceling extreme positions and forcing compromises on some surprisingly moderate and rational grounds. In a democracy, "gridlock" among opposing views is not necessarily bad. Americans—fortunate enough to have a system of contentious "checks and balances" built by our founders right into the DNA of our own national government—ought to understand this better than anyone else.

LEARNING TO LIKE SHIITES

As the new Iraq moves beyond its founding, however, one group will almost certainly end up first among equals.

And that is Iraq's Shiites—because they constitute around 60 percent of the population. This is portrayed in the Western press as an ominous fact, with constant reminders that it was Shiites who led the Khomeini revolution in Iran.

I see no reason, however, to be panicked by the idea of a multi-faction Iraq dominated by the Shia branch of Islam. To begin, very few Shiites have taken any part in the armed insurgency against the Coalition during 2003–2004. Indeed, the Shiites were thrilled to have Saddam toppled, and they have stepped forward cooperatively in large numbers to man the democracy councils, new military units and other institutions organized by the United States to point Iraq in a new direction.

As the guerilla war raged, both senior Shiite leaders and the rank and file all across southern Iraq showed a good deal of patience, forbearance and maturity. Potentially explosive events like the assassination of beloved Shiite moderate ayatollah Bakr Hakim (along with many of his followers) right outside one of Iraq's holiest mosques could have sparked fierce unrest. More than three hundred thousand mourners attended Hakim's funeral, which they could have turned into a rampage against other Iraqis or U.S. troops. But they resisted the temptation to rage. The appalling al-Qaeda bombings in March 2004 that killed hundreds of Shiite pilgrims at holy shrines were likewise weathered with impressive restraint. Most of the faithful grieved these tragedies responsibly, treating them as atrocities carried out by murderous outlaws rather than excuses for general uproar and abandonment of the non-violent path to a better nation.

Similarly, amidst U.S. confrontations with Shiite radicals like the firebrand Imam Moktada Sadr, many Shiite congregants and clerics have openly repudiated the extremists. Street demonstrations and popular revolts threatened by Sadr, for instance, have repeatedly fizzled. Each time he has discovered that he doesn't speak for most of the Shiite faithful, and that more moderate ayatollahs were secretly or openly backing American forces against him, Sadr has been forced to back down. I myself expect a bloody end to Moktada Sadr's thuggish career. But the idea that masses of Shiites are likely to follow him down whatever path he takes is, I believe, mistaken.

Ali Sistani, the Shiite grand ayatollah, has more authority in Iraq than any other single person. Yet even he is learning that in the emerging democratic Iraq, there are limits to his ability to dictate events. In Sistani's climactic spring showdowns with Paul Bremer and other Iraqi political factions over the transition to Iraqi control in mid-2004, the ayatollah eventually had to surrender on all of his major objections. His insistence on immediate direct elections was deferred. His requirement that the interim Iraqi constitution describe Islam as the sole source of Iraqi law was refused by other parties. And when he asked for alterations to two other provisions of the constitution after it had been accepted by all parties, the Kurds and Sunnis would not reopen negotiations. Even Sistani's fellow Shiites eventually decided to sign the document, despite his reservations.

These events have shown Sistani that he cannot force others to accept all of his positions on the form of Iraq's future government. And to his credit, he has so far given way when required. While negotiating hard with American authorities and other Iraqis on many points, the ayatollah has avoided threats and calls to violence. This is the spirit of compromise that is essential to democratic politics, and the Shiite leadership—contrary to some relentlessly alarmist spin generated by the American media—has so far demonstrated enough of it to keep movement toward a new Iraq on track.

In addition to this behavioral evidence, there is also attitudinal evidence of the relative moderation of Iraqi Shiites. When *The American Enterprise* polled a cross-section of Iraqis from four different cities in 2003 we found that, contrary to media impressions, the Shiites are noticeably more likely than others to reject theocracy as an appropriate form of governance for Iraq, more likely to criticize al-Qaeda and Osama bin Laden, and more likely to cite the United States as an attractive model for the new Iraqi government. In fact, Iraq's Shiites, despite being coreligionists with Iran's Shiites, preferred the United States over Iran's Islamist republic as a model for governance by a factor of six to one.

We hear a great deal about what Iraq's extremists want. But the American public knows comparatively little about what ordinary, everyday Iraqis believe and hope for. In Iraq as in most countries, there is a large silent majority, so popular opinion can't accurately be judged by listening only to squeaky wheels. We need to look beneath the roiling surface of attacks, demonstrations and explosions that dominate the daily headlines, and take time to examine the underlying bedrock of popular convictions. Which is exactly what we'll do in the next chapter.

4

WHAT ORDINARY IRAQIS WANT

A re everyday Iraqis glad to be free of Saddam Hussein? Are they on the side of the radical Islamists? What do they think of al-Qaeda foreigners coming to their country? What is their attitude toward the United States? What kind of government would they like for themselves?

These are some of the $64,000 questions about America's presence in the Fertile Crescent. Unfortunately, we rarely get hard information about what's in the minds of the large but often silent middle of Iraqi opinion. Instead, the answers proffered by reporters, government officials, experts and commentators are often merely guesses. We have had to rely heavily on anecdotal temperature-takings of the Iraqi public, and particularly on stories and images fed to us by the press.

And we all know that journalists have a bad-news bias: a thousand schools being rehabbed is not news; one school blowing up is a weeklong feeding frenzy. A peaceful religious march is a yawn for many reporters; a few maniacs cutting themselves with swords is an audience-attracting bonanza. Unless they are careful, journalists in Iraq unthinkingly gravitate to whatever is aflame; and in the process, they overlook the softer, deeper, and ultimately far more important story of the unfolding of a social and political revolution in the heart of the Middle East.

When I returned to the United States after my weeks in Iraq as an embedded reporter in the spring of 2003, I found the news about developments in the country to be increasingly puzzling. The postwar stories often seemed to be built on the flimsiest evidence. And they sounded much gloomier than was merited by my own experiences in the country, or by the reports I was continuing to get from the soldiers who were actually carrying out the nation's reconstruction. The disconnect became so acute that I decided to seek out some hard evidence as to where the truth lay.

I am fortunate to be a fellow at the American Enterprise Institute, one of the nation's foremost public policy think tanks in Washington, D.C., as well as editor of *The American Enterprise* magazine. Combining these resources, I wrote a questionnaire for the Iraqi public and commissioned a polling firm, Zogby International, to conduct the survey. Given the state of Iraq in the summer of 2003 this was not an easy task to pull off.

There is no nationwide phone system in Iraq, so all the survey questionnaires had to be administered face to face. We decided that if Americans were present we'd risk getting the answers the participants thought we wanted to hear, so only Iraqis were hired, supervised by experienced Lebanese pollsters. Respecting Arab tradition, only women were employed to question female respondents, again to avoid distortions from possible nonresponse or self-censorship.

We knew it would be easy to get misleading results due to wording problems, cultural differences or fears about publicly offering frank opinions in a country where just a few months earlier that could have gotten you killed. So I consulted with Polish and other Eastern European survey researchers about the techniques they had used right after the fall of the Berlin Wall to elicit honest answers from people who, in a similar way, had been conditioned to repress their true sentiments. In keeping with their recommendations, we kept the survey short, offered anonymity and avoided approaching people's homes — working instead in public gathering places. Zogby struggled to get the right regional samplings so we would have a fair cross-section of the country. The firm drew usefully on prior experiences polling under harsh conditions in places like Iran, Indonesia, Pakistan and Saudi Arabia.

We labored with Arabic specialists to make careful translations, modifying the text several times to avoid misunderstandings. One Iraqi warned me, for instance, that in our opening disclaimer promising to keep respondents' answers confidential, the Arabic word we used for "private" had an additional connotation of "secret." If you tell Iraqis in post-Saddam shell shock that you'd like to talk to them about something "secret," many will just turn away in fear.

In short, we did everything we could to make sure our results would accurately reflect the views of Iraq's multifarious, long-afflicted people. Our survey, which we launched in August 2003, was necessarily limited in scope, but it captured a nationally representative sample of Iraqi views in four disparate cities: Basra (Iraq's second largest, home to 1.7 million people, in the far south), Mosul (third largest, far north), Kirkuk (a Kurdish-influenced oil city, fourth largest), and Ramadi (a resistance hotbed in the Sunni Triangle).

Ours ended up being the very first nationwide scientific poll of the Iraqi public ever conducted. In light of how difficult it was to carry out, I know now why nobody else tried it earlier! Some of our intrepid fieldworkers in Ramadi got caught in crossfire; another group was chased by an unidentified car; the team in Basra was summoned by religious figures and questioned about the purpose of the study; and one of our supervisors was seized by Kurdish forces in Kirkuk and not released until a payment of money and several calls were made to local contacts.

But the information we obtained, which was released in *The American Enterprise* and the *Wall Street Journal,* and summarized by me in congressional testimony and many media appearances, ended up being highly useful in moving the Iraq debate further from fiction and closer to fact. The most important finding was (in a nutshell) that the Iraqi public is more sensible, stable and moderate than commonly portrayed. Like all societies, Iraq has its radicals, its optimists, its apathetic people, and a large mushy middle. But the country as a whole turns out to be not nearly so fanatical, seething, or disgusted with the United States as the actions of some extremists might make us believe.

First of all, Iraqis are optimistic. Seven out of ten told us they expect that both their country and their personal lives will be better five years from now. To American ears, this may not seem impressive. But keep in mind that nothing in Iraq's past justifies any optimism about the future. This is a country that has been on a horrible downward slide for decades; per capita income in the country fell to *one-tenth* its previous level during Saddam's reign. If so many Iraqis are now expressing hope, this is a sign they believe the regime change launched by America is fundamentally a change for the better.

The toughest part of reconstructing their nation, Iraqis told us by three to one, will be politics, not economics: they are nervous about democracy. Asked which is closer to their own view, "Democracy can work well in Iraq" or "Democracy is a Western way of doing things," five out of ten worried that democracy is specifically Western and won't work in Iraq. One out of ten wasn't sure, while four out of ten said it could work.

Since democracy is something brand new to the region, something no Iraqis have any local experience with, I regard this result as not unexpected and not especially troubling. Self-government is a concept that the people of Iraq will have to adapt to gradually. I wouldn't look for world-leading freedom right away, but if Iraq can develop even a rough democracy of the sort that we have helped set up in the Balkans, that will be a great improvement, and the foundation for future progress.

And when you peer beneath the surface, there are significant divergences on this issue. Sunnis were negative on democracy by more than two to one, but the majority Shiites were as likely to say democracy would work for Iraqis as not. People age 18 to 29 are much more rosy about democracy than older Iraqis, and women are significantly more positive than men. There seems to be more than enough confidence in the idea of democracy to get the process of self governance started.

NO NEED FOR NIGHTMARES

The next big question is: which direction are Iraqis likely to take as they chart their own course? Skeptics of Iraqi self-rule typically invoke three nightmare scenarios: 1) Iraqis will cling to Saddamism, or 2) the country will become a hotbed for al-Qaeda-style jihadism, or 3) Iraq will follow Iran down the path of mullah-ridden theocracy. Fortunately, our poll suggests that none of those worries is very likely to come to pass.

Almost certainly, there will be no Baathist revival—Saddam and his minions turn out to be enormously disliked in the country. We gave Iraqis a chance to let bygones be bygones by asking them whether Baath Party officials who committed crimes should be punished or whether it would be better to put the past behind us. A thoroughly disgusted and unforgiving public opined by 74 percent to 18 percent that Saddam's henchmen should pay for their sins. So forget about a Baath Party comeback.

The second nightmare scenario is that al-Qaeda-style terrorist organizations will proliferate in the new Iraq. But it turns out there's not much of a base there for the jihadist message. Many Americans don't realize, for instance, that al-Jazeera—the Qatar-based TV network that frequently serves as a mouthpiece for al-Qaeda chieftains—is not popular with Iraqis. They resent its longtime apologetics for Saddam's nasty regime.

To test al-Qaeda's appeal directly, we asked Iraqis what they think of Osama bin Laden. Of those with an opinion, 57 percent view him unfavorably, with fully 41 percent saying their view is *very* unfavorable. Iraqi women especially dislike him.

"But isn't it a serious problem that there's *any* support for bin Laden?" asked a friend who is a *New York Times* reporter. I reminded him we're talking about the Middle East, and that the sensible comparison is to popular opinion in places like Saudi Arabia, Egypt and Jordan. These are our closest regional allies, and even within their boundaries bin Laden is a folk hero to many people. The Middle East is hardly a land of moderation or Ameriphilia. I believe the attitudes expressed here by Iraqis are ones we can work with, as we do in other parts of the region.

Besides, when you look closer at the demographic cross-tabulations, you can see something interesting: the "very unfavorables" toward bin Laden outrank the "very favorables" by 2.5 to 1 in Mosul, by almost 4 to 1 in Basra, by 6 to 1 in Kirkuk. Only in Ramadi is the al-Qaeda mastermind popular—more than two thirds of his "very favorable" responses come from that single location. So this seems to be more an aspect of Sunni Triangle/Baathist estrangement from the United States (the enemy of my enemy is my friend) than real enthusiasm for bin Laden.

Even more importantly: as foreign jihadists have murdered increasing numbers of Iraqi civilians, police and respected public figures in the months since our August 2003 poll, Iraqi resentment toward terrorist groups has grown wider. Shiites and Kurds in particular (who jointly make up 80 percent of Iraq's population) have come to despise al-Qaeda after being repeatedly targeted by the group and its allies in ghastly suicide attacks on holidays, at family gatherings and in leadership meetings. With even more confidence than back in August, I suggest you can dispatch a "bin Laden romance" from the roster of potential Iraqi disasters.

The third mega-worry for Iraq is that the country could repeat the Iranian trauma by turning into an Islamic theocracy. Many of the commentators promoting this fear seem unaware, however, that Iraqis are actually quite secular. When our poll asked respondents how often they had attended Friday prayer in the previous month, fully 43 percent told us they had not been to mosque even once.

When we asked directly whether they would like to have an Islamic government, only a third of Iraqis (33 percent) said "yes." A solid 60 percent thought that people should be allowed to practice their own religion. One vital detail: Shiites, so often portrayed as self-flagellating ayatollah-maniacs-in-waiting by Western reporters, turn out to be least receptive to the idea of an Islamic government, saying "no" by 66 to 27 percent. It is only among the minority Sunnis that there is interest in a religious state, and even they are split evenly on the question. So the notion of an Ayatollah Khomeini rerun can also, most probably, be scratched off the Iraq critics' list of morbid fears.

All of this is reinforced by the results when we asked Iraqis to name the one country they would most like their nation to model its new government on. I carefully chose the alternatives offered in this question: Syria is not only one of Iraq's immediate neighbors but also the Middle East's other Baathist republic; if you like Saddamism, there's your model. Second alternative Saudi Arabia is also a neighbor, as well as the leading Islamic monarchy; for Iraqis seeking a king, it's the bellwether. Our third alternative, Iran, gave enthusiasts for a fundamentalist Islamist republic a place to rally around. For Arab nationalists there was fourth alternative Egypt, the lodestar of the Arab world. And our final option was the United States.

It's highly significant that the U.S. was the favorite model by far. Among those selecting one of our five possibilities, America was preferred by 37 percent—more than Syria plus Iran plus Egypt put together. Saudi Arabia ended up in second place, at 28 percent.

Again there were important demographic splits. Younger adults are especially favorable toward the United States, and Shiites are more admiring than Sunnis. Interestingly, Iraqi Shiites (who are coreligionists with Iranians) have little admiration for Iran's Islamist government: America is six times more popular with them than Iran as a model for governance.

Interestingly, the majority Shiites fell on the more moderate side in nearly all of the questions in our poll. The survey research data thus reinforce the conclusions suggested by Shiites' behavior—that they do not, generally speaking, constitute a force for radicalism. They turn out to be less likely than other Iraqis to want a theocratic government, more favorable toward democracy, more apt to pick the United States as the best model for government, and more negative toward Osama bin Laden. So why are they the bogeymen in so many tales about Iraq?

THE UN-FANATICS

Since our August survey, a number of other opinion polls have been conducted in Iraq. Here are some of the investigations I've tracked: a Gallup poll covering Baghdad alone, another canvassing of Baghdad by a respected British firm, several national questionnaires by Iraqi academics, one multi-city November survey commissioned by the U.S. State Department, an informal street poll by the *New York Times,* and a February 2004 nationwide poll commissioned by ABC, the BBC and TV networks in Germany and Japan. Despite very different methodologies and geographic coverage, the results of these disparate inquiries are generally quite congruent. In these polls, as in the one by *The American Enterprise,* the Iraqi public turned out to be quite optimistic, unambiguously glad to be free of Saddam, and (despite some mixed feelings) anxious to have U.S. troops stay in their country for a while as Iraqis establish themselves on a new footing.

For instance: When British pollsters working for *The Spectator* asked Iraqis whether America's "war against Saddam's regime was right or wrong?" 65 percent with an opinion said "right" and 35 percent said "wrong." When asked in the same survey what sort of governmental system they would like, the preferred choice among seven options was "British/American-style democracy," chosen by 36 percent. The second choice, pulling 26 percent, was "Islamic rule tempered to modern ideals." Only 6 percent of Baghdadis said they would prefer "Islamic rule in strict accord with the Qur'an."

When Gallup asked what condition Iraq will be in five years from now, compared with the condition before the arrival of Coalition forces, 67 percent of Baghdad residents said "better off," and only 8 percent said "worse off." Fully 62 percent stated that ousting Saddam was worth the hardships endured. Queried about how American troops had behaved, 58 percent of Iraqis said "well," while only 29 percent said "badly."

In October 2003, *New York Times* employees asked a mix of residents from three Baghdad neighborhoods about progress in reconstruction, or lack thereof. The *Times* reported that 85 percent said safety had increased in their area in the previous two months. And 60 percent stated that the Americans were doing a good job.

An eight-city survey by the Iraq Center for Research and Strategic Studies carried out after Saddam's December arrest found that 60 percent of Iraqis were "delighted" to see him detained. A majority said they want to see Saddam executed.

As I write, the very latest poll is the one conducted by ABC News with three other European and Japanese TV networks. Its most striking finding is that, when asked about "today's conditions in the village/neighborhood where you live," 70 percent of Iraqis say their lives are "good" at present, while only 29 percent say "bad." Asked to compare specific conditions with what prevailed just before the war, those interviewed said that "crime protection" was now "better" rather than "worse" (50 to 21 percent). Medical care also had gotten "better" rather than "worse" (44 to 16 percent). Other changes, according to

Iraqis: Electricity—43 percent better, 23 percent worse. Jobs—already 39 percent better, 25 percent worse than before the war.

People were also asked in this poll whether attacks on Coalition forces were acceptable to them. "Unacceptable," said 78 percent, with only 17 percent thinking otherwise.

This striking opinion evidence, with nearly all of the surveys I've cited overlapping in their moderate findings, suggests that Iraq is a manageable place. If the relatively small number of militants conducting sabotage and murder inside the country can continue to be dispatched to paradise or prison by American troopers, then the mass of citizens living along the Tigris-Euphrates valley eventually seem likely to make reasonably sensible use of their newfound freedom. "We will not forget it was the U.S. soldiers who liberated us from Saddam," said Abid Ali, an auto repair shop owner in Sadr City.

None of this is to suggest that the task ahead for Americans will be simple. Inchoate anxiety toward the United States showed up when *The American Enterprise* asked Iraqis whether they thought the U.S. would "help" or "hurt" their country over a five-year period. By 50 percent to 36 percent, they chose hurt over help.

This is fairly understandable: Iraqis have just lived through a war where Americans were—necessarily—flinging most of the ammunition. This may explain why Iraqi women (who are more anti-military in all cultures) show up in our data as especially wary of Americans right now. Though U.S. forces made heroic efforts to spare innocents over the last year, war is usually experienced by noncombatants as a curse.

Perhaps the ultimate indication of how comfortable Iraqis are with America's aims in their region came when we asked how long they would like to see American and British forces remain in their country: Six months? One year? Two years or more? The fact that 59 percent told *The American Enterprise* that Coalition troops should stick around for at least another year or two indicates that the radicals who are trying to drive them out immediately do not represent the views of average residents.

Incidentally, other polls come up with similar results. In a November 2003 Baghdad University study, 72 percent of interviewees said the U.S. military occupation is desirable and should continue for a while. A five-city poll released in January 2004 found that two-thirds of Iraqis have concluded that insurgent attacks show "the need for a continued presence of Coalition forces." Fully 71 percent of respondents said they would feel "less safe" if Coalition forces left immediately; only 11 percent said they would feel "more safe."

It's these views of ordinary Iraqis—much more than those of the extremists who excel at catching the ears and cameras of Western reporters—that we need to remember as we strive to establish an island of sanity in the Middle East.

UNPOPULAR INSURGENTS

Discovering that they usually die when they fight American soldiers, the guerillas have spent most of the last year preying on the weak and innocent—striking mosques, humanitarian agencies, hotels, political headquarters and other civilian targets. Their aim is to create an atmosphere of generalized fear, the better to destabilize society. The guerillas in Iraq have consistently launched their bloodiest strikes on religious holidays. In the case of the Irbil bombing that killed sixty Kurds, the two murderers were actually dressed as Muslim clerics.

These are desperate and retrograde military strategies; they win the insurgents no friends. Even before the end of 2003, it was already Iraqis who were bearing the brunt of guerilla attacks. This puts the insurgents on the wrong side of Iraqi opinion.

The best estimate by military intelligence officers is that the active resistance fighters never numbered more than about ten thousand Iraqis, and that by early 2004 their ranks had been reduced. The several thousand extremists plotting in the Sunni Triangle have no chance of winning militarily. Their only accomplishment is to create chaos.

The insurgents are strictly a negative force, who aim merely to wreck the transition to self-government and slow Iraq's climb toward economic prosperity. They are nihilists who hold nothing sacred. Their motto is "the worse, the better"—the slogan of radicals everywhere who hope that anarchy and civil war might leave an opening for strongmen like themselves who otherwise command little following.

It's essential to keep in mind that Iraq's insurgents have no platform, no winning message, no identifiable leaders. They don't represent a popular movement or enjoy any widespread support. They are simply well-armed fringe fanatics.

In short, these are political criminals, leftovers of the old Arab power blocs. They are feared by many Iraqis, but not respected, trusted or liked. And they are finding it hard to swim among the Iraqi public or find holes in which to hide.

One might reasonably ask why sensible Iraqis don't stand up more visibly to be counted. I see two reasons. One, Iraqi culture (particularly as it has been warped by Saddam) doesn't encourage individuals to speak up and hold fellow citizens accountable. In my next chapter I look at the problem in detail. Second, decent Iraqis are afraid. They remember 1991, when we came to their country but didn't follow through. People who backed change at that time suffered horribly under the bullies who re-exerted control after we failed to step in.

We are going to have to prove to moderate Iraqis that we'll not abandon them, British prime minister Tony Blair points out. For "they know their own street, unused to democratic debate, rife with every rumor, and know its volatility. They see the Western media. And they ask (as the terrorists do): Have the Americans and British the stomach to see it through?"

Evidence that the guerillas lack popular legitimacy can be seen in the *fatwa* condemning "any act of violence against Iraqi state government workers, police and soldiers" issued early in 2004 by twenty-one Iraqi imams in response to guerilla car bombings. Another indication of their unpopularity is the fact that insurgents have had to pay bounties to recruit attackers on American soldiers. Bribes of $250 to $1,000, with bonuses if there are actual casualties, are used to entice individuals (usually poor

Sunni fundamentalists) to perpetrate attacks. These fees have had to be hiked at various times to provide sufficient incentive; and as papers found on the person of Saddam Hussein when he was captured reveal, the insurgents are running out of the cash required to keep this mercenary fighting active. The need to pay bribes to keep cannon fodder in the field is the reason guerillas resorted to numerous bank robbery attempts during the winter, including the spectacularly failed effort in Samarra on November 30, 2003, that left fifty-four guerillas dead.

Many of the most violent participants in the insurgency are foreigners. There aren't large numbers of foreign jihadists in Iraq—Brigadier General Martin Dempsey estimated, in March 2004, that there were perhaps one hundred foreign terrorists in Baghdad, organized in perhaps six cells. Major General Charles Swannack reported in January 2004 that his 82nd Airborne paratroopers had killed or captured around fifty foreign guerillas in a little over half a year of counterinsurgency, and he estimated in March that there was a total of perhaps fifty more still operating in the Fallujah/Ramadi hotspot west of Baghdad. In addition, one Army estimate is that an average of eight or so foreign fighters cross into the country each week.

What they lack in numbers, though, the foreign terrorists make up for in viciousness. Most of Iraq's more horrific and bloody attacks—including nearly all the suicide bombings—are considered almost certainly the work of non-Iraqi jihadists. The capture of Hassan Ghul as he crossed into northern Iraq in January confirmed al-Qaeda's active involvement in the country. Ghul reported directly to Khalid Sheik Mohammed, one of the leading planners of the September 11 plot, and he was carrying documents pointing to al-Qaeda's involvement in scores of attacks on the Coalition and its Iraqi allies.

Think of the current situation in Iraq this way: A psychological contest is under way for local loyalties. On one side are remnants of an unpopular regime, reinforced by unpopular foreigners, who merely wreck and kill in ugly ways, especially at religious and humanitarian sites, frequently on holy days, with most of the victims being innocent Iraqis. On the other side are American forces who have, on the whole, been quite gentle and forbearing. (It's not unusual now for Iraqis to criticize Americans for being *insufficiently* ruthless in dealing with the insurgents.) And those American forces are just beginning to gain access to a $32 billion infusion of aid offered up last year by the United States and thirty-four other contributors. These fresh resources will equip the Coalition to speed the rebuilding of the country and demonstrate even more clearly to Iraqis who is on the side of progress and human kindness.

And you know what? That's a pretty good position from which to prosecute a war against minority guerillas.

No guerilla war is easy. But there is no Ho Chi Minh trail pumping fresh poison into Iraq, and with each passing season there will be fewer weapons in the hands of fewer guerillas with less and less money to spend.

Meanwhile, new economic and political freedoms are unfolding across the countryside: Cell phone and satellite TV usage are exploding. Fully 1,500 schools have been rehabbed, and teacher salaries increased by a factor of about 15. One million cars had been imported as of April 2004. Pharmaceutical distribution has gone from almost zero in 2002 to around 20,000 tons annually. And at least 318 local democracy councils are now up and running.

There are currently more than 170 newspapers published in Iraq, and broadcast media are proliferating. Traffic clogs streets, stores are bustling, a restored currency is in circulation, and most goods and services have exceeded their prewar levels. About 10,000 miles of irrigation canals have been cleared of weed infestations. Large territories that are home to millions of Iraqis—places like Arbil, Basra, Kirkuk, much of Baghdad, and vast swaths of countryside in the north and south—are stable, basically peaceful and beginning to bubble economically. World Bank and other economists estimate that the country's total output of goods and services will jump by a huge 33 to 60 percent in 2004.

And in March 2004, all of the nation's nonviolent political factions agreed to the interim constitution and a governing schedule that will bring Iraq's first-ever open elections by February 2005. Cumulatively, these innovations amount to a social, economic and political *revolution*. One that makes the blood-feuding insurgents look more and more unattractive to normal Iraqis with each passing week.

5

THE CHARACTER TEST

Having argued that much is encouraging in the current practice and future potential of democracy in Iraq, I now want to point out some of the stiff challenges that lie ahead. In particular, I'll present observations by the American soldiers I talked to, plus some of my own, as to how cultural and moral factors may complicate the rebuilding of Iraq.

We Americans sometimes tend to think it is "parchment" that ultimately keeps us safe and free. Every schoolchild learns that our written laws, our political institutions, and ultimately our Constitution are the bulwarks of liberty, the difference between our nation and others that exhibit much less fairness, freedom and prosperity. That's true enough. But it's not the whole explanation.

My time in the war zones of Iraq reminded me that there are influences on how successful a nation is that are even deeper and more important than constitutional underpinnings. In particular, there is the influence of individual character, as shaped by moral teaching and religious practice among the citizenry. I'll illustrate this with examples of recent successes and failures in the land of the Tigris and the Euphrates.

■ ■

Being rich in natural resources like oil and water, and having an educated and ambitious citizenry, Iraq's long-run prospects are reasonably bright. But in the course of launching Iraq as a free nation, U.S. soldiers are finding they have to work around some significant obstacles. One is widespread corruption.

"You can't necessarily trust people. There is a lot of dishonesty here," warns Lieutenant Michael Eitelman. Americans know about the chronic looting and thievery that break out across the country whenever policing sags. But the problem is deeper than that. "Whoever's in charge of a given project may take whatever they want. You've got to watch very closely," says Eitelman. "We've had lots of turnover in the police, the army and the governing councils as we've gradually weeded out bad apples."

Ethical problems have contributed to Iraq's societal woes in many ways. American soldiers found, for instance, that they had to closely supervise new recruits to the Iraqi police and army during house searches to make sure they didn't steal things. In one sector of Baghdad I covered, Iraqi lawyers hired to record claims of war damages for possible reimbursement were found to be fabricating cases in collaboration with false filers, with whom they would split the compensation payments. I mentioned in Chapter Two how an emerging leader of a democracy council in southwestern Baghdad had to be arrested for channeling council money into his own pockets.

Once uncovered (often thanks to tips from more upright citizens), these infractions generally fade. But there are many bad habits to reverse. "It's pretty much expected in this culture that you will make kickbacks and practice cronyism and nepotism. Practices in public life that would get you prosecuted in the U.S. are almost a norm here," says Major Jim Murphy, the burly, shaved-headed brigade chaplain for 82nd Airborne soldiers stationed in the Baghdad region. "If someone gives you a contract, you're expected to give them a payment in return. There's no clear tradition of just finding the best person for the job."

Major Mark Stock bluntly describes another stumbling block in the way of good governance and healthy civic life in Iraq: "Almost every day here I run into a number of Class A liars."

"I only know one Iraqi who I am certain has never told me a lie," reports Colonel Fuller at the end of his stint overseeing about one-quarter of Baghdad for most of a year. "Dishonesty and corruption are real problems here. There are crooked politicians everywhere, and there are other cultures, like in Central and South America, that have something similar to the Arab practice of 'baksheesh'—whereby you've got to give a 'tip' just to get work accomplished. But those things are a plague here. The former regime was an extreme kleptocracy. Everyone stole from everyone. Corruption became the only way to survive. We've made an example of some people we've caught in corrupt behavior, stealing, and so forth, and I believe we're making progress. But you don't dare assume people will do the right thing."

LOOK TO WASHINGTON, NOT D.C.

A related dilemma, suggests Major Brett Jenkinson, a tall, thin executive officer who has been in Iraq for eleven months, is that "there is no tradition of selfless national patriotism in this society at all."

Captain Ken Burgess, the company commander who was active in setting up advisory councils in many Baghdad neighborhoods, agrees: "This is a pretty cutthroat society. The order of priority seems to be: Self. Then family. Then tribe. Then associates. Country comes way down the list. The sense of unselfish service, and of nationalism, is something I haven't seen much of."

"The idea that 'He who would be the servant among you would be the greatest of all,' that's not a concept I've seen modeled in this culture," adds Chaplain Murphy. He notes that Iraqi Christians, a tiny minority in the country, are considered by other Iraqis to be less corruptible. "Even Saddam used to say: 'The Christians don't steal.' This is apparently a main reason that Iraqi Christians have influence in professional fields far out of proportion to their small numbers—they are considered honest."

An American observing Iraq at this critical juncture in its national history might be forgiven for muttering to himself: "Where is this nation's George Washington? Where is the leader of high integrity who will put the people's interests above his own?" Ayatollah Sistani, the powerful Shiite religious leader, is by all accounts a modest and incorruptible man, but some of his more extreme religious and political views stray outside the Iraqi mainstream, and his odd refusal to meet with Americans and other Iraqi factions except indirectly, through intermediaries, prevents him from becoming instrumental in Iraq's rebirth. Meanwhile, many Iraqis who have been active in the national Iraqi Governing Council have been too concerned with pursuing their own selfish interests and establishing their own positions, businesses and perquisites, rather than attending to the nation's urgent needs.

I must report that the disappointments include Ahmed Chalabi, the U.S. favorite who was seated next to Laura Bush at the President's 2004 State of the Union Address. Military intelligence officers tell me that the information brought to them by Chalabi's Iraqi National Congress has, contrary to his grandiose promises, been mostly worthless. Too often it has even seemed cooked to suit his parochial purposes. This extends way back to the INC's involvement in exaggerated prewar claims about the state of Iraq's nuclear and chemical weapons programs. Chalabi has also failed to generate a loyal following among responsible Iraqis. Indeed, in the February 2004 national poll sponsored by ABC, he was the only politician of any stripe whom significant numbers of Iraqis described as someone they "don't trust at all."

More fundamentally, Chalabi has let down many who hoped he would emerge as a principled, forward-looking and positive leader. In his public statements and actions, Chalabi has been quick both to criticize the United States and to heap demands on American representatives. He and some other Iraqis whom one hoped would rise to be the natural leaders of their post-Saddam nation have very rarely solved problems themselves, offered useful services, or otherwise taken charge. When I hear these Iraqis whiningly complain that they need safer neighborhoods, fresh entrepreneurial efforts, cleaner streets, restocked hospitals, a reopening of Baghdad Airport, elimination of looting and black-marketeering, and other salutary changes, my main reaction is: Why stretch out your hand and ask America for all this? Why not organize your citizens to do these things for themselves?

Don Walter, a retired federal judge who was part of an expert team that toured Iraq to assess the condition of its legal system, had this to say to officials in Baghdad's Ministry of Justice at the end of his inspection: "I have talked to hundreds of you over the past five weeks, almost everyone educated and privileged. What I have heard is what you want from us, how the Americans have to fix this, and give you money and equipment, protect you from your own. You need to do some of these things for yourselves. If you are relying on us to do everything, you are going to be sadly disappointed."

Numerous soldiers involved in civic reconstruction in Iraq told me that some of the country's difficulties reminded them of the welfare culture that the United States has been trying to break down in its own inner cities—particularly the dependency syndrome that leads people to look automatically to someone else to solve their problems. But in Iraq, passivity and dependence appear not just in pockets, but across broad swaths of society. As we passed through the filthy yards and trash-strewn streets of Iraqi residential districts on various errands, U.S. soldiers would often puzzle: "Why don't they at least pick up their own garbage? That doesn't cost anything, and it would improve their lives overnight."

Recognizing that unproductive attitudes lie behind many of Iraq's current troubles, our military governors are emphasizing the importance of cultural change, not just the spending of money. As one officer commented wisely, "We could pour billions into this place and make no long-run difference if we don't change attitudes and behaviors. So that's one of our biggest pushes—to get Iraqis to take responsibility for their own fate."

THE RESPONSIBILITY GAP

These problems are compounded by debilitating political fantasies that impede some Iraqis (and many Arabs in other countries) from taking responsibility for their own societal failures. Think of the insistent claims, believed even by many educated Arabs, that it was Israel's Mossad that felled the Twin Towers; that the American Army was being annihilated by heroic Iraqi resisters in the spring of 2003, as Baghdad Bob claimed in his Alice-in-Wonderland news conferences; that Baghdad's national museum was looted by American soldiers rather than by Iraqi thieves; and that the man captured in the spider hole on December 13 was merely a Saddam double, drugged by the CIA. "There's a persistent, destructive, paranoid mythology that clouds clear thinking," states commentator Andrew Zaplatynsky, "almost like a whole society intent on believing that O.J. is a victim."

Writer Steven Vincent, who has recently spent weeks exploring Iraq, has described the angry shame some Iraqis feel over the fact that foreign power was needed to free them of the tyrant Saddam:

One waiter admonished me, "You should have waited just a little longer. We would have risen up and over-thrown him ourselves."

When I asked why the Iraqi people hadn't toppled Saddam before, other Baghdadis claimed that the tyrant had support from "outside" forces—most notably the Jews....

At a small social function one evening I spoke to an Iraqi woman who expressed excitement over the fall of Saddam. Yet in almost the same breath, she declared, "I hate the Americans." ... When asked how she expected Saddam to fall without the hated U.S. soldiers, she looked at me miserably. "I know," she said, "and you can't imagine how that humiliates me...."

Iraqis, I found, do not blame themselves for Saddam. To them, he is like a gunman who burst into their homes, seized their families, and terrorized the neigh-bors—until the police finally stormed in and drove him out. Now, standing amid the ruins they say: "We weren't responsible for the maniac. You took it upon yourself to remove him. Thanks, but how soon are you going to repair our house?"

High Iraqi officials are in denial on these matters as much as people on the street. Sometimes they act as if the United States initiated the long chain of events that brought their country to its current troubles. Take, for instance, the February 2004 statements of Sami Mahdi, of the Supreme Council for the Islamic Revolution in Iraq, in an interview with German television. "We are grateful to the Americans for getting rid of Saddam, but would have preferred to do it alone. The U.S. shouldn't have acted without a U.N. mandate. That was bad form." He went on to criticize the U.S. for being "tactless" in Iraq: for "searching women," being "disrespectful to tribal leaders," and sometimes even "entering houses without knocking." Coming from a man who had many colleagues killed by Saddam and his henchmen, these prissy legalistic objections are bizarre. And his almost humorous statement that "we helped the Americans get rid of Saddam by not working against them" can only be taken as a psychological dodge from the fact that it took outside intervention to set his country aright.

POLITICS AND RELIGION

What are some of the cultural factors that have dragged Iraqi society down? One is simply political misrule. "Iraqis have been totally dependent upon the government for everything for thirty-five years. As a result, some of them never grew up. They never learned to take the initiative and resolve things themselves. They want us to fix every little problem for them, and we keep saying 'you've got to do that for yourself,' " reports Major Murphy, the brigade chaplain.

Other social institutions that could have provided alternative leadership also failed. Many of Iraq's mosques were co-opted by Saddam Hussein. He demanded their fealty, installed many of their religious leaders, then rewarded sycophancy with state funds for buildings and social programs.

"The initial model of a Muslim cleric I started with was that of a Christian pastor," Murphy explains. "As I got to know the imams across Baghdad, I realized that was totally wrong. They don't function the same way, or have the same motivations.

"Many of the imams have their fingers in real estate, business, whatever. In particular, there is a complete entanglement of religion with politics here. Often they're one and the same thing.

"One local imam, Sheik Moyad, tried to take over this area during the summer. He was seizing property and buildings, then reselling them or installing squatters. He was stealing generators. He was kidnapping opponents. He was taking prisoners at gunpoint, and bullying his neighbors. He was trying to build a large neighborhood power base and financial empire.

"He was essentially operating like a Mafia don. After he threatened several of our commanders, we finally had to arrest him. He's on trial this week—charged with extortion, murder, storing weapons in his mosque, and other crimes. I testified yesterday." (Moyad was later found guilty by an Iraqi judge, and sentenced to seven years in prison and a $1,000 fine.)

"One of the things that has bothered me," Murphy concludes, "was discovering that clerics would often absolve their fellow Muslims of terrible things even when we had caught them dead to rights. In many cases they'd rather leave a bad Muslim in place than let a Christian exert any control over him. They just refused to accept that a Muslim could be held accountable by a Christian 'infidel.'"

This attitude has been symptomatic of Islamic societies across the globe. Reverend Ian Sherwood is the minister who conducted a memorial service for the thirty innocent people killed in the November 2003 bombing of a bank and the British Consulate in Turkey. After the service he remarked, "I'm appalled that I've not received any statements from a Muslim teacher anywhere in the world to express sorrow or reconciliation." When ethical leadership and human solidarity are needed in international affairs today, many observers are left wondering: Where are the shepherds of the "religion of peace"?

INDIVIDUAL SCRUPLES, COLLECTIVE SUCCESS

In *Human Accomplishment,* his book examining the roots of great achievement, the social scientist Charles Murray came to a conclusion that surprised him, as a nonreligious man: After years of historical study, he discovered that the key to the flowering of science, high art, enlightened governance and many other good things in Europe (later flowing from there to other parts of the world) was the Christian religion's influence on individuals and societies. As Murray recently summarized in *The American Enterprise:*

> Christianity's revolutionary potential begins with its core teachings that all human beings are invited into a personal relationship with God, that all individuals are equal in God's sight regardless of their earthly station, and that salvation is available to all who believe and act accordingly. It is a theology that empowers and energizes individuals as no other philosophy or religion had ever done before.

An emphasis on individual righteousness, personal character and accountability before God, doesn't just give Christians ways to draw nearer to the divine. It also provides them with valuable tools for living more wholesomely on earth. George Washington argued in his Farewell Address that "morality is a necessary spring of popular government," and he advised Americans to keep a tight grip on their Christian faith. Many times as I observed failures of citizenship in Iraq, I wondered if the troubles I was witnessing were exacerbated by the lack of a comparably influential moral framework.

Clearly, Christian religious belief isn't the only path to individual accomplishment and societal success. But one of the wonderful overflow benefits of Christian faith seems to be that it encourages personal and social behavior that makes it easier to create a just and stable society. Nations which lack Christianity's ethical infrastructure may face a harder climb to the good life.

This does not, of course, mean that all Americans are good citizens and all Iraqis unscrupulous. As Alexander Solzhenitsyn reminded us, the line between good and evil runs directly through the heart of every human being. Selfishness, dishonesty, corruptibility, ethnic hatred, violence—these are sins that every person and all cultures will wrestle to control until the end of time. My point is simply that Americans can count their blessings that they have a religious and civic heritage that unambiguously condemns and reduces such behaviors.

And as a practical matter, it is only because the basic integrity of most American troopers can be taken for granted that our Army is able to succeed at the reconstructive work it's carrying out today in Iraq. "I'll be honest with you," Major Stock tells me, "we pretty much have *carte blanche* here. This is a war zone and we are the armed, absolute rulers. If we want to arrest anybody, for any reason, we can." The controlling factor is moral restraint among soldiers and officers who are trying to do the right thing. In the course of their searches, soldiers regularly uncover piles of cash, and they are dispensing millions of dollars worth of U.S. currency and goods from their own stocks in order to get Iraqi society working; here again it is personal integrity, not the loose controls that come with wartime, that has prevented widespread abuse.

Given the opportunities and temptations, the general absence of financial, revenge-based, sexual or other improprieties by young American soldiers in Iraq is encouraging. These GIs are hardly perfect, but under difficult circumstances they've demonstrated a capacity to avoid graft, cruelty and advantage-taking. I've watched soldiers calmly and politely search the homes of insurgents who had killed their buddies just days before.

The basic decency of American soldiers is, I suggest, the main reason the U.S. military is succeeding in Afghanistan and Iraq, while the Soviet Red Army failed miserably in similar battles amongst Islamic rebels in Afghanistan and Chechnya. By committing atrocities and failing to build up wholesome alternate social institutions, Russian soldiers only managed to stir up ever more impassioned resistance. American fighters, on the other hand, pacified Afghanistan (which swallowed the communist invaders whole) in a period of months, and are having far more success in Iraq than the Russians in Chechnya, even though the Iraqi assignment is a much tougher one.

For all of this we can credit U.S. Army discipline. But we must thank even more the religious and civic traditions that temper selfish and sinful impulses and channel them into more productive directions, resulting in young Americans who are mostly good and trustworthy citizens. In countries where moral scruples are not as successfully implanted into the breasts of citizens by institutions of religion and culture, it isn't impossible to create a good society, but it's certainly a lot harder.

THE POWER OF LINKED ARMS

It also interested and surprised me that most American soldiers were able to keep their spirits so high in Iraq. "We never bottomed out. Attitudes stayed pretty positive throughout," Lieutenant Eitelman told me just a couple of weeks before he completed his year-long deployment. A soft-spoken native of Abilene and graduate of Dallas Baptist University, now headed into the Special Forces, Eitelman credits the character of his fellow soldiers: "I don't know where you're going to find this quality of great men anywhere else in the world. They may exist, but I don't know where."

There has been a lot of reporting about the strain placed on our soldiers by the six- to twelve-month deployments to Iraq. Obviously, these deployments can be very taxing, especially for soldiers with spouses or children back home. But tours of this length are not unprecedented. During Vietnam, *all* soldiers spent one year in country. In Bosnia, a twelve-month deployment started out as the norm; six-month tours began in 1996. Back in World War II, fighting units were employed for "the duration" of the war. The same soldiers who started out in North Africa in 1942 also fought in Italy and in Normandy, and then crossed the Rhine in 1945.

More than any other, the concern I heard expressed by soldiers was not that they would be in Iraq for some unbearably long period of time, but rather that something might happen that would prevent them from winning the fight and making their mission a success. One officer wrote me in October 2003:

> We must show the world that we have the stomach for the ugly realities of a righteous war. I believe with all my heart that this effort is critical to the survival of this region, the position of the U.S. as a world leader, and the spirit of our fighting forces in the future. The only way we can lose this war is if we lose our resolve. Specialist Babin, who remains hospitalized with brain and internal damage, Specialist Bermanis, who has lost three limbs, or Specialist Ross, who lost his eyesight and leg saving a young Iraqi, would never forgive us for giving anything less than our all from here on.

One of the things that has kept the morale of our fighting forces from sinking is their closeness and loyalty to each other. "There's so much shared experience. We depend on each other tremendously over here. Because of that, you get tight even with very different people, guys you might never become friends with under other circumstances," explains Lieutenant Eitelman.

Most of the GIs I observed in Iraq were able to remain surprisingly loose, calm and unconflicted under pressure. There was even a fair amount of humor. In the most dangerous camps right at the Halloween peak of the guerilla attacks, some paratroopers went trick-or-treating in their underwear and combat boots.

Of course there are some obnoxious officers, despotic sergeants and lonely privates in our Army. But every time I spend a few weeks with our soldiers in a war zone, I'm struck by how tight-knit and companionable most of them are with each other. There is a great deal of warmth and fondness among troopers at war. When things get rough, they pick each other up, both figuratively and literally; I myself have been a beneficiary of soldiers' generosity too many times to even count. When I latch on to a unit I often feel, even as an outsider, the strong sense of being included, watched out for and backed up that makes our fighting units so effective.

The forced intimacy of military life may explain why there are fewer cliques and separations and group resentments in our Army than in most other sectors of society. The schisms that are so common in our ethnically divided urban neighborhoods, among rival religions, between political partisans (think Red vs. Blue America), amidst jealous corporate departments and on college campuses (where "black" and "white" tables in dining halls are the norm)—these are comparatively rare in our military. The emphasis is on issues that unite rather than those that divide. The Army has proved its ability to dissolve many of the barriers of race, age, region and economic class that can be so prickly in other settings.

After some years of writing about military folk ranging from service-academy cadets to infantrymen, it's clear to me that there are two groups that our current armed forces attract in disproportionate numbers. One is composed of people who grew up in strong families and communities where they developed a powerful sense of human fellowship and a willingness to sacrifice for the larger good. The other group comprises people from damaged families where this very same feeling was absent—and hungered for. I've met a significant number of soldiers who were children of divorce, or otherwise suffered a withered or unsettled home life, who then as young adults went seeking the sense of belonging and purpose they had missed growing up. For these, the Army can become a substitute family.

For both of these groups, the impulse to link arms with others and serve a higher cause in the military ends up benefiting all Americans—and, in this case, also many Iraqis and other people who aspire to live in peace.

6

MILITARY-INDUSTRIAL COMPLEX

After two weeks in Baghdad, I'm now in a Black Hawk bound for the Fallujah region, which has pretty much been Ground Zero for the Iraqi resistance over the last year. Helicopters shot down in these environs have yielded some of the worst single-day losses of life in the war—including the nine men who died when their medevac copter was rocketed on my first day here two weeks ago. Helos now fly only at night in this locality, and they maneuver evasively, in total blackout, to make themselves difficult targets. Airplanes leaving Baghdad International take their own countermeasures—they fly tight corkscrews as close to straight up as their engines will carry them, not straying from the immediate vicinity of the airfield until they've risen high above the clouds.

As soon as our chopper lifts off, we begin to bank and dip, zig and zag. It's a clear night and we are flying low, so the swooping curves allow good views of Baghdad out of the large Lexan windows on either side of the bird. After about half an hour of this aerial juking amidst the turbine roar and the percussive overhead pounding of blades on air, we suddenly drop to the ground. It's pitch black outside; dust is whirling. The copilot yanks open the side door. To communicate over the din, I quickly scrawl "St. Mere?" (the name of my landing zone) on a pad of paper and shine my LED pin light on it. The pilot nods his helmeted head. I grab my pack and step out into black ink.

I can see nothing. Then a glow, perhaps a cigarette, off at one corner of the landing zone. I walk gingerly toward the spot, unable to pick out anything in my surroundings. There I find a kindly lieutenant in a Humvee. I was supposed to be met by someone able to take me to the next battalion I am visiting, but no one has come. Army contingency 101: the crossed signal. "Don't worry, I'll bring you back to the brigade with me," he says, "because this is just an air strip, and once we leave there's no one here." I nod my head gratefully.

Arriving unannounced at the 82nd's 3rd Brigade headquarters, I fall into the hands of the Public Affairs Office, and with a bit of a sinking feeling I roll out my sleeping bag and crash for the night. Sure enough, the next morning I'm snared in a little spider web of Army bureaucracy. Permission needed; this is classified; you can't go there; that takes time; I'll seek approval; yadda yadda yadda.

I need to get out of this planning and supply terminal and into the field with some infantrymen. I press hard on each of the three people in the PAO office. Luckily some officers I crossed paths with during the war last spring come over, carrying copies of *Boots on the Ground* for me to sign. The sergeant who controls my fate relaxes a little. And he sees that I'm going to pester him to death if he doesn't ship me over to the action quickly, so we agree on a busy schedule for the next few days and start to enjoy each other's company. Turns out to be a nice guy.

OUR NEEDLE-NOSE SYNDROME

At breakfast I catch up with a helicopter pilot I met over here last March, and two other fliers who are eating with him. One of them is an Air Force jockey with a patch on his flight suit that says "T-bolts Rule," so I assume he flies an A-10 Thunderbolt, the old, ugly, ponderous, but exceptionally effective flying brick house that soldiers love for its ability to float in low over a battlefield and pulverize enemy troops, vehicles and buildings.

"Nah, too slow," he says, curling up his nose. "My F-16 squadron just uses the nickname, 'the Thunderbolts.'"

This preference for needle-nosed supersonic fighters is overwhelming throughout the Air Force. And in an era of guerilla war against terrorists hiding along city streets, this is a real problem. Designed to shoot down Soviet aircraft or pulverize ground targets from high altitudes, our fighter jets have become sleek, expensive movie stars in search of work. They are very good at plunking a few large bombs on a tank or radar or command post, and there will always be important tasks of that sort to be carried out in any war. But their basic ground-attack weapon is a 500-pound bomb, usually delivered to a GPS coordinate with an accuracy that could just as well take out the house across the street as the one the pilot intended. That bang is simply too big and too imprecise to use against insurgents shooting at friendly soldiers from inside a school building. And fighter jets can carry only a small number of these bombs; then they must return to a base (in this region, often far away, and always hard to procure and defend) in order to reload.

To prosecute its war on terrorists over the next decade, the U.S. military badly needs a different set of aerial assets. We need less emphasis on fighters. We may need more heavy bombers; the U.S. currently has only 60 B-1 bombers (little more than half of them ready for combat most of the time) and 21 B-2 bombers (likewise, only a portion of them combat-ready). We rely on 76 B-52s, which are still great workhorses. But the very youngest B-52 was built in 1962, and these planes are currently scheduled to remain the backbone of our heavy bomber fleet through 2040.

We certainly need more unmanned drones (and trained operators) capable of hovering over battlefields collecting intelligence—and occasionally launching missile attacks— without endangering a pilot's life. And we need a larger fleet of transport aircraft to ferry infantry and their equipment to the many points across the globe where conflicts are erupting.

We need additional planes like the A-10 and the AC-130 gunship that can fly at low altitudes to obliterate fighters directly engaging U.S. soldiers and Marines, without producing friendly casualties. Though you'd never know it from our plane-procurement priorities, ground attack has been the main mission of the Air Force in pretty much every war since Korea, and these heavily armed planes once again proved invaluable in Iraq and Afghanistan.

More generally, we need less emphasis on breakthrough airplane designs, and more effort at producing improved airborne conventional weapons, avionics, guidance systems and precision battlefield-control systems that actually destroy enemy targets. As Stephen Budiansky points out in his new book *Air Power,* the U.S. military has long spent 80 to 90 percent of its acquisition budgets on new platforms (planes, vehicles, ships) and only 10 to 20 percent on the munitions that they carry. The comparatively simple satellite- and laser-guided bombs that have become so critical to our warfighting successes over the last decade were starved of funding for many years. The modified Boeing 707 JSTARS planes that have proved so valuable as overhead controllers of ground fighting had to struggle for every scrap of funding, and it was mostly owing to luck that two experimental prototypes had begun flying in time for their important debut in the first Iraq war. Even as we've recognized the importance of precision weapons systems, we still have a long way to go in equipping our existing aircraft with the most modern targeting devices, night/all-weather navigation systems and "smart" munitions.

The trouble is, much of the Air Force disdains these unglamorous tasks. Its pilots want to strap themselves to wild mustangs tearing through high pastures, not draft horses and sturdy mules clearing bottomlands of stumps and rocks. Aircraft like those I've mentioned above still receive only a tiny portion of Air Force acquisition funds; meanwhile there are three new supersonic fighters in the pipeline—an enhanced F-18, a new F-22, and a new F-35 designed to battle heaven-knows-who for air supremacy. (To be fair, other service branches are also buying expensive superweapons that have little use in a post-Soviet world

Urban Warfare   A convoy of soldiers from the 10th Mountain Division and the 82nd Airborne snakes through a Fallujah neighborhood bordering the Euphrates River. The .50 caliber machine gun overlooks watchful U.S. fighters, Iraqi civilians, an AP news photographer (black helmet)—the full panoply of guerilla-war elements.

Meeting of the Minds Colonel Kurt Fuller and Lieutenant Colonel Dave Haight (back to camera) mull how to handle religious extremists.

Deadly Blast   Crater marks the location where an IED consisting of three artillery shells wired together killed two paratroopers of the 82nd Airborne just days before their return home.

Confiscating a Kalashnikov   Under American rules, every Iraqi family is allowed one military rifle and one ammunition clip. This AK-47, found wrapped in clothing under a house, was seized for exceeding the limit.

Operation Desert Swarm   After a frigid pre-dawn ride, paratroopers from the "Red Devil" brigade prepare to execute a series of raids and searches in the vicinity of Uwaylim.

Knuckle Rapping Sheiks Riyad and Akram are questioned by Colonel Kurt Fuller and warned not to repeat incitements to violence in their Friday sermons.

The Men of Karb Degla A military intelligence officer, seeking the perpetrators of a deadly roadside bombing one week earlier, takes names among the clansmen of Karb Degla.

New Recruits　A U.S. Army Ranger trains new members of the Iraqi Civil Defense Corps, who will carry out much of the anti-terrorist work in the country once Iraqis are in charge.

Goodbye to the Old Iraq   Back-scratching Sunni sheiks, after nursing the loss of their privileged position under Saddam Hussein for
nearly a year, finally request a meeting with the American Army.

Democratic Iraqis   Two members of the Dawrah Advisory Council discuss rehabilitation of a former palace that is to become a district social center. Dr. Nasreen Hidar Qatar, left, a physician and Kurd, also represents hundreds of thousands of her neighbors on the Baghdad City Council.

Going In Soldiers line up to enter the house of a suspect in an early-morning raid in Baghdad. The man with his head covered by a ski mask is an Iraqi-national translator.

Night Visit   The house of an Iraqi suspected of recruiting drivers to transport explosives to Fallujah is searched by paratroopers for hidden weapons.

Eye Opener Chaplain Jim Murphy of the 82nd Airborne says he learned that Muslim clerics are different from Christian pastors during his year in Iraq.

The Cement Factory Colonel Mike Oates, left, Lieutenant Colonel Tony Layton, center, and a Civil Affairs officer tour an industrial complex where the U.S. Army hopes to get vitally needed jobs and production back on line.

Cannon Maker Out of Work An employee at the artillery factory putters at some small fabrication, while plant managers contemplate the transition to capitalism.

The Artillery Factory Through an interpreter, Colonel Oates promises skilled Iraqi machinists in an idled defense plant that he will do his best to find them work, and that they should "have hope."

Justice Dawns   The sun rises on four Iraqi men captured at the homestead of a former officer in Saddam's presidential protection force.

A Morning's Work Battalion commander Marshall Hagen supervises a large cordon-and-search operation by several hundred of his men in a rural area between Baghdad and Fallujah.

Stash Buster A soldier from the 1st Infantry Division uses a metal detector to search out arms stashes buried underground.

Mixed Bag These Iraqi children were delighted with the American soldiers who visited their farmstead. But some older brother or other relative may feel differently: immediately in front of their home, the road was pocked by three ugly IED craters.

Passing the Torch Marines (note the distinct camouflage) who command units selected to replace the Army in March 2004 are briefed by two of their Army counterparts on aspects of the local insurgency.

Dumb Loyalist   When Jassim Khudari was captured in a dawn raid, his letters professing "deep love" for Saddam were still in his home, along with multiple false identity cards and a device for triggering roadside bombs.

Do It Yourself   A paratrooper instructs new Iraqi police officers on how to search vehicles at a traffic checkpoint.

Inspection Tour Captain Chris Cirino, right, and the commander of the Fallujah Iraqi Civil Defense Corps, left, flank General Ricardo Sanchez, commander of all U.S. forces in Iraq.

Commuting in Fallujah   In a city where traveling in force is the
only way to avoid fatal attacks, an armored Humvee can provide
some protection.

Cityscape U.S. soldiers are mystified that Iraqis passively let garbage accumulate in their yards and streets.

The Religion of Peace? General Sanchez examines an improvised rocket launcher found with al-Qaeda tracts just outside a Fallujah mosque.

History in the Making   The Fallujah Provisional Advisory Council as they prepare to hold the city's first democratic vote, to elect a leader.

Nation-Building Fighters   Immediately after U.S. soldiers orchestrated the historic city council meeting to select a president, their
exit convoy was hit with an IED. This photo was taken from two
trucks back just seconds after the detonation.

After the Blast Paratroopers storm into a residential compound and frisk all those present after an IED planted directly across the street rocked their Humvees. It turned out, however, that these family members were terror victims just like the soldiers.

On the Beat   In certain parts of the Sunni Triangle, soldiers patrol city streets that can be friendly one moment, then turn deadly at the next corner.

Raiding a Propaganda Shop   Soldiers from the 82nd Airborne and the 10th Mountain Division use a battering ram to force entry into a record store that has been peddling violent anti-Coalition tapes and CDs.

Checking the Inventory   Arabic-fluent troopers carefully search for intelligence and evidence inside the shop selling insurrectionist recordings.

Getting Pinned One week before leaving Iraq after a full year of combat service, paratroopers of the 325th Regiment line up to be decorated with their Combat Infantry Badge.

Dutiful Soldiers   A C-130 military aircraft carrying the author and
35 American GIs out of Iraq also transported the body of a fallen
comrade killed in the line of duty.

where terrorists are the new enemy. Does our Navy, for instance, really need a new class of attack submarine?)

THE WAR ON CHOPPERS

Another clear aeronautical disappointment in the war on terror has been the helicopter. The usability of choppers was limited somewhat in Afghanistan by the thin, high-altitude air and jagged mountains. The Iraq war exposed a great many more weaknesses.

Maintenance has been a nightmare in the sandy environment. And desert landings often turn out to be dangerous because the rotor wash kicks up so much dust the pilots can't see the ground. "Lots of times I haven't been able to see well and ended up with a hard landing," one Black Hawk medevac pilot told me. "One of our guys almost flipped his bird recently because he couldn't tell that he was sliding laterally as he touched down. It's a miracle we haven't had even more people hurt."

"This is definitely a hard place to fly helicopters," another pilot admitted. In the first sixty days of the war there were seven fatal helicopter crashes, claiming the lives of thirty-seven servicemen. A number of times during my first embedded tour in the spring of 2003 (during prime dust-storm season), I saw the 82nd's entire Kiowa fleet grounded for lack of visibility. Even with clear skies, the combination of night-vision goggles and touchdown dust can be so difficult that night-time flying has to be eliminated.

Now an even greater danger—ground fire from surface-to-air missiles, RPGs or small arms—is pushing in the opposite direction. Scores of passengers and pilots have been killed when their helicopters were shot down from below. (Over a year, a total of sixteen choppers have been lost in Iraq.) As a result, in many areas pilots now try to avoid flying during the day, and when they have no option, they make sure they move constantly at top speed. Forget single-point reconnaissance, convoy cover, hovering over infantry, or regular patrolling of a cordon-and-search boundary. In the most restive parts of Iraq, staying put for the length of time those kinds of missions require invites a fiery crash.

But of course, eliminating such missions defeats much of the purpose of helicopters; those things are supposed to be the bread and butter of helicopter warfighting. And it isn't just the light-skinned Kiowas and utilitarian Black Hawks that have proved surprisingly frail and vulnerable, but also large cargo copters and even our fearsome Apache attack helicopters. Having apparently recognized the vulnerability of even the most expensive high-tech choppers, the Army announced in late February 2004 that it was canceling its $39 billion Comanche program. Instead, it will upgrade and modernize the 1,400 helicopters already in its fleet.

"We have infrared transmitters intended to confuse heat-seeking missiles," one highly experienced helicopter pilot told me, "but they don't work well when somebody shoots from underneath us. We need another beacon down there. And we have a built-in defensive system that spits out flares and chaff to distract incoming missiles—

but it's push-button activated on most of our helicopters, and the majority of hostile shots we don't see, or we see them too late to react. It needs to be activated automatically by computer."

If technical solutions can't alleviate the weaknesses revealed in Iraq, helicopters will have proved to be much less useful than planners of anti-terrorist actions may have wished. In the meantime, many pilots are skittish. "The number of helicopters shot down has surprised us," concedes a pilot and company commander. "These days, flying is just no fun at all."

BRICKS AND MORTAR

Fallujah is a city of nearly 400,000 souls, with more Saddam partisans per capita than about any other place in Iraq. A considerable number of the electricity pylons dotting the surrounding desert have been sabotaged. Remnants of high-voltage cables hang loosely off each side of every tower like sagging arms—neatly clipped off about seven feet above the ground, as high as a looter stripping the steel and copper wire can reach with his snips. They remind me of trees at home in the Adirondack Mountains that have all been trimmed to a similarly precise height— the level a winter-starved deer standing on snow can reach as it cranes for buds and other forage.

I'm in an armored convoy headed for a vast acreage that is home to two cement factories, a brick production line and a tile plant—one of the main industrial sites in greater Fallujah. When the U.S. Army first arrived, this hulking but broken-down facility employed only 200 workers, turning out dribs and drabs of product. After a little tinkering it now provides jobs to 750 workers, but still operates only in fits and starts. If it were up and running at full production, it could employ 2,200 people in a city desperate for salaries.

One main shortcoming is electricity. At full bore, the complex would require up to 16 megawatts of power; it currently gets 1 megawatt, and occasionally loses its juice altogether. The Army began to supply generators, but discovered that the large units needed would consume lakes of diesel fuel that are simply not available in this war zone.

The other pressing shortfall at the cement plant is miserable maintenance and a lack of spare parts. The machinery in the various buildings is in tatters from years of neglect. The Iraqi engineer leading us through the factory explains that they have adequate cash flow to buy parts and replacement equipment, but need permission from the minerals ministry for every transaction—a constant chokepoint.

An Eastern European now working for the Coalition Provisional Authority tells me that Iraqi heavy industry under Saddam was very similar to command-and-control communism at its worst. "Eeet's oonbeleefable!" he fulminates, "zey can't do anyseng vid out ahprooval." By the time the Berlin Wall fell, the economies of Eastern Europe had already evolved somewhat toward more freedom and flexibility, he notes, so the demands of a market economy were not wholly unknown there. But right up to spring 2003, Iraq's large industries were still run by commissars stamping make-believe five-year plans.

This interesting tour (led by locally based U.S. Army officers who have been working with Iraqi managers to assess the plants and get them functioning again) includes a high-level delegation from the CPA that is surveying the economic potential of the area. Members include Jacek Kwasniewski (a Pole who directed much of his country's privatization of industry after the fall of communism, now planning Iraq's private sector development for the CPA); a very sharp mechanical engineer and colonel in the Romanian army who is one of the CPA's experts on state-owned industry; technical people from the State Department and the U.S. Agency for International Development; and several U.S. Army officers assigned to the CPA.

The team is led by an energetic military officer — Colonel (soon to be General) Mike Oates, who as the new whip-cracker for the CPA's chief operating officer, Keith Kellogg, is charged with getting Iraq's gears turning. "You know, of the $18 billion the U.S. is going to be investing in Iraq this next year or so, $12 billion is going into construction. That means cement and bricks. So there's a large potential market for what these folks make," he states. Through an interpreter he questions one of the plant's engineers and learns that the facility could turn out 1,000 tons of Portland cement per day at peak capacity. That's a lot of foundations and walls.

"But before we get excited and start pushing resources into a place like this, we need to figure out a few things," Oates muses out loud. "First, what would it take, technically and financially, to get this place operating again?" A sergeant who has been working with the managers says the best estimates for a full rehab come to more than $10 million.

"Alright, then second we have to figure out if the local electrical infrastructure could support the plant running at full blast. If not, there's no use in fixing things up. Third, we need to be sure they have customers. Can they market their product if they get geared up? And, last, we need a good assessment of whether this is economically feasible. Sure, we could help them do it, but would the number of jobs produced be worth the investment it would take? Or would we be better off spending those dollars at a bunch of smaller projects elsewhere?"

Spoken like a good businessman. But in this case by a man wearing a helmet, desert fatigues and a 9mm pistol instead of a three-piece suit.

GETTING BABYLON BACK IN BUSINESS

Next I have a conversation with Kwasniewski, whose intelligence and economic acumen impress me. Not only is he a Ph.D. economist and ex-government minister who was a primary engineer of Poland's shift toward capitalism, but he later founded one of the most successful investment banks in Poland. His firm orchestrated $6 billion in transactions from 1996 to 2002, including the privatization of the Gdansk shipyard.

"From the beginning I wholeheartedly supported the effort to free Iraq," he said. "Then I was asked to join the CPA as a Polish representative, to work particularly on the privatization of Iraq's state-owned industries. The technical part was not hard. But privatization is only one-quarter technical; the main obstacle is garnering enough political support to push through the necessary alterations. That is always tricky. Last fall the privatization effort in Iraq died, at least for the moment, because we failed to earn the support of the Iraqi Governing Council.

"But, you know, that's not such a big problem — because Iraq never had a lot of state-owned industries. Outside of oil, only 5 to 7 percent of Iraqis worked for state companies. The vast bulk of the country's employment and non-oil GDP is in the private sector. So privatization isn't essential. What *is* essential is helping Iraq's small private businesses grow. The entrepreneurial spirit and energy in this country is enormous; businessmen just need better conditions and standards: credit standards, labor standards, legal certainties, an environment that encourages private business.

"And Iraq desperately needs investment—which will pour in quickly once a predictable set of rules is in place. For a quick boost I am recommending micro-loans to small businesses. An estimated 2.5 to 3 million Iraqis work in irregular or underground mom-and-pop enterprises. Keep in mind that the entire Iraqi paid labor force is 7 to 8 million. With modest loans, many of those extralegal entrepreneurs could become legitimate and join the on-the-books economy.

"Established businesses in this country carried an awful dead weight during Saddam's rule. All major firms had to give 10 percent of their revenues each year to the president and his cronies, and they had to accept the installation of Saddam's friends and family members into their offices, drawing large salaries, setting policies, interfering in many ways.

"Of course private business will survive anything; it can never be stamped out. But great damage was done to Iraqi enterprise. This needs to be cured. I am hopeful that Iraqi émigrés might help. Many have become successful businesspeople in the West. As some of them return, they will bring not just money but something much more important: Western ideas of business and management."

The combination of Iraqis' own efforts and the diligent economic pump-priming that American soldiers are carrying out has already brought significant progress. International reporters repeated over and over during the long, hot summer of 2003 that Iraq's unemployment rate was then a miserable 60 percent. Unfortunately, none of them are reporting in the spring of 2004, as I write this, that Iraq's jobless rate has already been cut by more than half, to under 30 percent—perhaps under 20 percent, some economists estimate.

Though they may not have those kinds of figures at their fingertips, many Iraqis recognize the economic efforts being made on their behalf. Just as we were leaving the cement plant, a threadbare man walked up and handed me something rather precious in the middle of this barren desert: a large orange aster blossom, plucked from some unseen corner of this industrial ruin where a hardy plant must have survived from the more prosperous pre-Saddam past.

Who says Iraqis didn't greet Americans with flowers? I got one. Even in Fallujah.

IN THE ARMORED CARPOOL

Saturday had provided me a good look at the predicaments and possibilities of Iraq's mercantile sector. On Sunday the CPA team and I burrowed deeply into an even more troublesome part of the country's economy: Saddam Hussein's military-industrial complex—in all its Stalinist squalor.

Our full-day trip took us to an artillery design and manufacturing center, an optical-sight factory, a plant for making shell casings and other facilities for producing war materiel. They were clustered in a series of huge compounds out in the desert, in the middle of nowhere; to get there we would pass through the center of Fallujah.

Ambushes are frequent and fierce in Fallujah, so any trip into the city requires serious combat preparation and contingency planning. With a large group of MPs in gun trucks as escort, we are traveling in force today—a convoy of seven Humvees, most of them armored, and about thirty-five men in all. To keep some distance from dangerous roadside bombs, the drivers straddle the line down the middle of the highway, pulling into the proper lane only at the last second when oncoming traffic necessitates.

"This particular vehicle's armor has been well-tested recently," says the driver of my truck. "About a week and a half ago we were hit with an RPG right in the middle of Fallujah. Luckily it glanced off our rear and did little damage. A little while before that we were blasted by an IED. Three 155mm artillery shells wired together went off when we were about eight feet away. Fortunately they buried it too deep. So here we are." The inch-thick glass of the windshield is crazed with a swirl of cracks from the IED's shock wave and deep pits where pieces of shrapnel hit. It's a good thing for this Wisconsin boy that he wasn't driving a regular Humvee.

A longtime citadel of the Baath Party and the Iraqi military, Fallujah is unquestionably more sullen than Baghdad. Stony faces stare as we roll through garbage-filled streets as squalid as any I have seen on five continents. The oft-attacked U.S. soldiers operating in this harsh city seem to have been hardened by their environment. They are cold, a little numb, rarely waving to the children who give them a thumbs-up. On buildings along the main street I notice the only anti-American graffiti I've seen in Iraq. One traffic circle we enter is positively ringed with ugly IED craters; the sergeant hollers to the gunner protruding from our roof hatch to crouch down into the truck while we pass through it.

The downtown animus is not universal to the area, however. In the extensively farmed rural areas along the river just outside the city we get many waves, smiles, friendly faces and shouted greetings. I note once again how compartmentalized Iraqi society is by region, faith, class, education and history, and how divided many of the nation's sub-peoples are on critical issues.

Back out in the desert we pass one of the largest storage points in Iraq for seized ammunition. "Keep in mind that Iraq actually possessed more conventional ammunition than the entire U.S. military," says Colonel Oates. "There were originally something like six thousand ammo dumps in this country."

Army specialists are sorting huge quantities of every-thing from bullets to ballistic missiles—destroying large stocks every day and recycling the rest for future supply of the new Iraqi army. Major General Swannack notes that "some of the caches we're dealing with are miles long and wide, containing thousands of tons of ammunition. To assist us in the reduction process, we've hired fifty local Anbar truckers and employed over seven hundred Iraqis—making the province safer for all of us." By the beginning of 2004, over 22,000 tons of ammo had been detonated in Anbar alone. "Yesterday I had a huge smile on my face as I personally blew up a hundred tons of ammunition out in western Iraq," grinned Swannack in the first week of January. "That made a big boom for the future of Iraq."

DUEL IN THE ARTILLERY FACTORY

At last we roll up to today's first destination: a massive artillery-tube fabricating facility. It seems the Iraqis acquired specimens of the top howitzers from China, the United States, Russia and other places, stripped them down, then reverse-engineered hybrid weapons combin-ing the best features of each. "They produced some excel-lent cannons this way," reports the U.S. artilleryman leading us through. Their research-and-testing program was run in the first building we enter—one of a series of football-field-sized industrial caverns we will pass through this day, many of them filled with enormous presses and milling machines and 20-ton lifting cranes. This is extra-ordinarily expensive equipment, European mostly, generally 1980s vintage. A company of soldiers from the 82nd Airborne's 3rd Brigade lives on the premises to prevent looting, but it's obvious that everything has been neglected for some years, and disorder rules.

Small knots of workers still show up every day, mostly standing around doing nothing or working fitfully on maintenance and piddling fabrications. They are here because the state-owned enterprise continues to make small assistance payments to them. (The funds come from the overarching Iraqi ministry, operating under CPA oversight.) They also show up because three thousand families who have depended directly on this factory for their livelihood are nursing hopes that some sort of production will resume here in the future.

There are messy heaps in all the yards, much broken equipment, a lack of spare parts, many shortages of power and supplies. But there remain enough machines, raw materials and skilled workers here to turn out goods; this is still one of Iraq's preeminent industrial facilities. The trouble is, the one product they specialized in—howitzer barrels—can no longer be produced in a demilitarized Iraq.

There are civilian goods (like hydraulic cylinders) that use similar production techniques. But the management is paralyzed by the idea of making independent contracts and selling to someone other than the Iraqi defense ministry, long their sole customer. As we walk the factory floor with the director and several engineers and supervisors, it's clear that while technically competent, they are utterly cowed and baffled as to how they should operate in the post-Saddam era.

Urged repeatedly by the visiting CPA officials to go find customers they can manufacture products for, they answer over and over, "I don't have permission for that. How would I get approval from the Military Industrial Commission?" One of the Eastern European advisors splutters: "Forget permission! If you have a customer, just make an agreement. Do you know people who might want to buy products from you?"

Manager: "Yes! A man wants us to make the cylinder for jacks."

CPA: "You have the expertise and the material?"

Manager: "Of course."

CPA: "Then do it! Don't ask someone in a Baghdad ministry who might reject the idea. Just make a contract."

Manager: "I must know who we are part of now. Who am I accountable to? Where must the money go if I sell something? Will somebody come along in two months and criticize me, saying 'Who allowed you to do such a thing?'"

MARKET JITTERS

Not sure if they have the freedom to do business independently, and deeply risk-averse after many years under a brutal dictatorship, the managers of this state-owned enterprise are afraid to head down the new road of making and selling things for a market. This has been a cumbersome bureaucracy for so long it will not be easy for the men in charge to shift gears.

"I have gone to the oil ministry, the ministries pro-
ducing steel and glass, to see if we can do work for them.
They tell me, 'Oh, you are under the Ministry of Military
Industry. We cannot work with you.'"

"You should look for contracts outside of the government," suggests one CPA official.

"I must have government-to-government contracts,"
comes the answer. "I cannot compete making auto parts.
Small private shops, many using looted equipment they
took for free, will give a better price."

"But all your equipment is already paid for. And you
have plenty of raw material lying around here for you to
work with. Just give a good price and start working," suggests a U.S. military officer.

"Right now all my workers are state employees. They
receive payments just for sitting here. I cannot get them
to do extra work unless I can pay them extra. There is no
incentive." At this point even the Eastern Europeans begin
shaking their heads.

A second manager has other reservations: "I need some
rules. How much do I reinvest into the company? How
much for profit-sharing to the employees?"

"For now, you just need to pay your workers, make
repairs, and pay for your materials," answers one of the
82nd's officers who is laboring to get this facility operating again. "Then put the rest in the bank. We'll take the
next step somewhere down the road. The important thing
is to start producing. And you must have open books, so
we can check all expenses and payments."

One looming conflict for the managers is the temptation to sell off the decommissioned howitzer barrels and

other steel in their scrap yard. That has quick cash value. But it is also, for the near term, their only source of raw material recyclable into saleable goods. An even more short-sighted possibility is that valuable machinery will be liquidated on the international used-equipment market. This could line some pockets in a hurry, but it would cripple the plant's ability to produce in the future.

Some large 1990s-era Swiss fabricating implements are sitting at curbside near the factory entrance when we arrive. "Those weren't here when we came last week," warns one lieutenant colonel. "Probably some managers profiteering right under our noses, maybe with the complicity of the ministry. We've gotta watch this or they'll strip the whole place out."

Just before we leave the artillery plant, Colonel Oates gathers a circle of several dozen workers around him and, with an Army interpreter, tells them he will return within a week or two with a team of technical experts. They'll analyze some of the civilian uses to which the manufactory might best be redirected. "We will help you get working again," he says, as the Iraqi workers crane to see his face. "Have hope."

POWER TO THE PEOPLE

Next we travel a short distance to another vast, walled factory. This is a facility for turning copper, zinc, tin and other metals into ammunition casings. The location is currently guarded by two different, mutually suspicious groups of Iraqis—tribal guards who watch the outer perimeter, and officers of Iraq's new Facilities Protection Service who are posted at the buildings themselves. A U.S. first sergeant in charge of this area tells us that the top priority of each group seems to be to make sure nothing on the property ends up in the other's hands.

This particular check and balance appears to be working, for there has so far been no raiding of the several million dollars' worth of raw metals that a preliminary U.S. military survey found in inventory here. The true figure might be even higher. Like many of Iraq's military-industrial sites, this one includes very extensive underground facilities, only a fraction of which the American soldiers have been able to search; most of the chambers are locked and the troopers are stretched too thin to be fooling around with forcing their way in.

In any case, the difficulty here is not raw materials or spare parts for the machinery, and the production line happens to be in a reasonable state of repair. The issue is electrical power: the plant needs 15 megawatts. It currently has none at all—there just isn't enough in the area to allot it any.

At present, Iraq has barely more than half the electrical generating capacity it really needs. In disfavored areas, Saddam's regime used to starve the civilian population of electricity so it could be rerouted to military-industrial priorities like this place. Today, the Coalition sends all available power to Iraqis where they live, and it may be a year or two before enough additional current comes on line to fully restart large-scale operations like this one.

Since so much ink has been spilled on the subject of Iraq's energy supply, I'd like to point out that as this book is released, barely one year after the beginning of the war, Iraq's total electrical generating capacity will be 50 percent more than the country's prewar peak. Iraq's oil production is likewise on the verge of reaching new heights. Amidst the disorder and active sabotage of a war zone, those are large accomplishments. (And let's remember that both were achieved primarily thanks to extraordinary exertions by the workers and management of companies like Halliburton—that ever-so-popular pincushion for partisan pricks.)

It's also intriguing to note that, although they have usually been reported as evidence of Iraq's sickness, today's electricity and fuel shortages could just as easily be described as healthy consequences of Iraq's progress. One reason the electrical grid is being stressed is because Iraqis are buying so many new appliances, boosting demand for current. (Thirty percent of the population had purchased satellite TV by spring 2004.) Likewise, new buildings must be heated, and more gasoline is being burned as millions of vehicles are imported into the country and people start driving more. Brownouts and gasoline lines are certainly things U.S. administrators need to avoid as much as possible, but when they are occurring because of the rapid expansion of Iraqi consumption, they should not be crudely characterized as gloomy symptoms of economic failure. They are challenges created by progress and good news.

As for military industries like the ammunition plant, there is no reason to restart them even when power is available unless they can be adapted to make civilian goods rather than war materiel. It happens that the sheets of brass and copper these particular lines produce could readily be redirected to domestic purposes. So relatively soon it may become a priority to shunt some electricity to the furnaces, rollers and stampers we see arrayed around us. Certainly the military and CPA men visiting today would dearly like to see this plant's 1,200 jobs reappear. That would give the men of this notably restive region something to do that's more productive than sabotage and mayhem.

IRAQI IMPORTS

As we've been tooling across the deserts of western Iraq all week long, I've been jumping out at every pit stop and walking the shrubby wastelands with my eyes glued to the ground. "Whatcha lookin' for?" a number of soldiers ask me. I tell the ones I think will understand that I have a nine-year-old son who recently started collecting bugs, and that I'm keen to find him something creepy from the dusts of Babylon. I even carried in my backpack that requisite of good insect collectors everywhere: a killing jar (just a small plastic container with a tight lid that contains a paper towel soaked in nail-polish remover). If I can slip some unwitting Middle Eastern specimen in there, I'll have a pickled prize to take back to my budding young entomologist.

There are some strange vermin in Iraq. The soldiers like to recount their experiences with camel spiders, some of which are as big as a fist, very fast moving and fond of empty boots as overnighting spots. Lots of GIs have stashed captured camel spiders and scorpions and lizards in cookie tins, boxes or plastic bags, and attempted to get them to fight. No luck—it seems that only humans spar for fun. The insect that soldiers fear most is actually a tiny, nearly invisible sand tick. It burrows beneath the skin and lays its eggs, creating huge festering sores that can quickly rot the flesh in ugly ways. If the infection gets into your bloodstream, you will die fast.

When I was here back in April 2003, I saw some very weird scorpions and stinging centipedes and two-inch-long flying ants that would thrill any grade-schooler. But now it's Iraq's winter, and all the darn bugs seem to be hibernating. Everywhere I go, I scan the ground with all the fatherly enthusiasm I can muster; but since arriving this January, I haven't seen so much as a decent-looking fly.

I'm beginning to worry I might go home empty-handed when I get lucky on this warm, sunny afternoon out in Saddam's weapons district. Suddenly I spot two black beetles heading for what looks like their home hole. Nothing flashy, but they are big and shiny, and better than facing an expectant young boy with nothing in my jar. Unfortunately I'm in the middle of taking notes and photos, and I don't have anything at hand to catch the critters with.

But I know how to spring in an emergency. So just as they are scooting down the entrance to their den, I jam my fingers deep into the sand and clamp my fist shut. I can feel enough wriggling to know I got something. As the rest of the group of Iraqis and soldiers I was walking with disappear into a building across the lot, I decide I'd better sort this out later. So I pluck out my handkerchief, dump my load of sand and beetles into it, and quickly tie a knot. As they claw their way to the surface, I can see that, yup, I've captured two creatures. I have to baby my parcel all day long to avoid smashing the goods, but that night when I pull out my killing jar, there are two nice little dime-sized treasure bugs—which I promptly dispatch to Allah and then stow for the trip home. Victory.

WEAPONS SCIENTISTS IN WATERTOWN

Our day's final stop is the community that U.S. soldiers call "Watertown" (for its large water tower that protrudes as a landmark above the plain, and in homage to the upstate New York town where the Army's 10th Mountain Division is based). The military installations we've been visiting are plunked in the middle of a vast, barren desert that would make the monastic scientists of Los Alamos's Manhattan Project feel right at home. To house the weapons researchers, engineers, machinists and managers working at the defense plants, and to keep them quiet under a watchful eye, Saddam built a gated town for their families to live in. It's a completely self-contained community of about 2,500 households, with its own stores, gas station, car repair shops, villas and apartments that are at the top of Iraqi standards. The much-better-than-normal housing and some expensive cars seen on the streets are clear evidence that this was a bastion of privilege.

But now these members of Iraq's science intelligentsia are mostly out of work. Colonel Oates tells an aide that a team needs to be brought out here to interview these technocrats and catalogue their science and military research skills. Brainy weapons specialists must not be allowed to drift away to high bidders on unfriendly shores.

And Watertown's residents have worries beyond unemployment. The ethnic schisms that haunt other parts of Iraq are appearing here. It seems that the poorer locals living along the river have always resented the interlopers, from all over Iraq, who enjoy the plum living conditions of this planned community. The locals are now threatening to seize and occupy the prime housing—which they claim sits on their land. "Go back home, carpetbaggers," they taunt. If civil war were to come and Coalition forces were not around to prevent incursions, Watertown's elite rocket scientists worry, they might lose their homes, as they have already lost their coddled professions.

Not surprisingly, this is one more place where American soldiers receive friendly waves from the streets.

7

GUERILLA LESSONS

Okay: I'm ready to make a commercial for Apple's iBook computer. For free.

As I sit on an Army cot in a small concrete building I'm occupying with five soldiers, writing late in the evening, I hear mortar fire starting to head our way. First shot: not near. Second and third shots: still not too near. Fourth shot: about the same. Fifth shot: I can hear it whistling almost from the moment it leaves the pipe. That's a bad sign. I lean away from the window and turn my face to the wall. A very loud explosion, very close.

I jump to my feet to take cover in the center of the building. But I forget that my laptop is plugged into the improvised wall socket the Army has wired up. Crash! My computer drops four feet onto concrete. And bounces. This is not good.

I'm on my knees lovingly retrieving the plastic and silicon rectangle from the floor. I agonize over which would be worse: dismemberment, or the mental death of losing my journalist's "weapon," and perhaps weeks of working and thinking.

The screen is black. The machine is shut down completely. I hold my breath and press the "on" button.

It restarts. I have lost about an hour of writing, but many days of prior work are perfectly intact. Thank you, Apple engineers. And damn the Iraqi insurgency.

The men of the 82nd's 319th artillery battery seem to share the latter sentiment. A few minutes later they begin counterfire with their 105mm howitzers. Boom, boom, boom never sounded so good.

FOLLOWING THE INFANTRY

The brigade headquarters where I have slept the last two nights is in a special compound originally built for some of Saddam's most favored foreign partisans—members of an Iranian terrorist organization called the Mujahideen-e-Khalq. Violent Marxists and thus enemies of Iran's current clerical regime, they defected from their country and received shelter under Saddam. From Iraq, they plotted against the Iranian government (Iraq's hated adversary), and paid homage to Saddam by doing some of his dirty work. They supported themselves financially by, among other things, making black-market sales of scrap metal from the huge piles of military detritus that litter the landscape—wreckage from the Iran-Iraq War and the failed takeover of Kuwait that in places stretches literally to the horizon.

The American troops already had more than enough on their plate when they first reached this area some months ago, so there were no arrests of the Iranians, just a quick "get out of town" ultimatum. By local standards, the Mujahideen lived like moguls. The walled main compound from which the Army ejected them includes extensive gardens, a large theater, marble paving on the plazas, even a palm-fringed duck pond with towering fountains that the 82nd's Iraqi caretaker turns on once in a while, lending a startling glamour in a country where I have rarely been tempted to use that word. It's quite a contrast from my previous billet—the raw Camp Falcon, where 82nd soldiers were in the middle of carving a headquarters out of an abandoned industrial site in Baghdad, amidst the gummy, ankle-deep, boot-sucking mud brought by winter rains. In comparison, the (aptly French-named) Camp St. Mère clearly rates *luxe* on the Iraqi bling-bling meter.

But now I'm being picked up bright and early by the men of 1st Battalion, 504th Regiment—the "Red Devils." I'm back with the infantry. In the words of my transport crew, the transition from St. Mère to their Camp Mercury is like "heading off to the redneck stepchild's house." I actually find it a comfortingly familiar layout: a few concrete buildings, lots of gravel, a bank of Porta-Johns, some noisy generators and tents.

We're close enough to the brigade headquarters that our food gets trucked over three times a day from their kitchens. A large complex of refrigerator trailers and food-service buildings surrounds the St. Mère chow hall, and here the typically cheerful Bangladeshi and Filipino kitchen workers that the Pentagon's private contractors have hired to staff camps all over Iraq churn out the fuel for the soldiers' bodies. The food is pretty fair, and quite varied. There are lots of weird but satisfying dishes, reflecting the ethnic mélange of humans assembled hereabouts: curry-flavored spaghetti bolognese, Mexican fajitas with fillings that make you think of Chinese food, bread pudding that resembles no recipe known to any American from the South.

In the camps that don't have their own contractors on site to do the cooking, precooked food is delivered in huge insulated coolers, and soldiers assigned to KP duty add little Americanizing fillips to each meal. One day, the truck carrying our evening dinner rolled over in a ditch, spilling the prepared dishes. Signs posted on the mess tent announced an hour's delay, which most of the soldiers used to work up an even heartier appetite by lifting weights in the exercise tent. When we returned to the mess, we were greeted by a substitute dinner made of hundreds of eggs apparently cooked in muffin tins. "Egglets" the troopers called them, popping them into their mouths like big white marshmallows.

To help patrol the roads around Camp Mercury and monitor for IEDs, and to lend some heavy firepower to certain operations, there is a detachment of armor here out of Fort Riley, Kansas. That's always a bit of an oddity for paratroopers (the tanks, that is, not Kansas), and in the beginning the M-1 crews gave lots of cab tours to infantrymen who wanted photos of themselves posed on an iron horse to send home. An Abrams can roll at 60 miles an hour and ride "smooth as a Cadillac" across almost any terrain, according to one driver. With 70 tons of mass, they don't need to worry about shock absorbers. But in the course of barreling hundreds of miles across Iraq, often on paved roads, the crews have worn down truckloads of tank treads. I enjoy watching them install fresh treads, change engines or do other massive maintenance work as easily as you or I might change our Buick's oil filter.

These are dominant weapons, invulnerable to almost anything they would normally meet on a battlefield, so the Camp Mercury tankers were buzzing about an explosion that had recently popped the turret right off an M-1. Pretty much a one-in-a-million lucky hit, everyone agreed. But even the rakish, mustachioed fifteen-year crew chief spinning yarns for me about some of his best shots admitted that he prayed most times he ventured out on the treacherous roads. "No use in fussin'. All I can do is trust in the good Lord," he tells me.

Off in an opposite corner from the tankers is the "Red Devil Roof Inn"—the detention tents ringed with concertina wire where the two companies operating from this location can hold prisoners for up to 72 hours. Hundreds of Iraqis have been processed through this facility since the battalion arrived in the summer. About a quarter of them usually get released after a few days; the rest are sent to the brigade level for further interrogation. From there a hard core goes to nearby Abu Ghuraib prison, the country's principal lockup, which sits about an hour west of Baghdad and currently hosts about 6,500 guests of the U.S. government.

At this level the Coalition considers the prison to be "full," though Saddam, less fastidious about humanitarian issues, reportedly packed 40,000 enemies of his state into the main jail—40 or 50 to a cell. He also carried out many executions at Abu Ghuraib. In the fittingly gloomy light of dusk I visited the death chamber, where prisoners were hanged two at a time, then cut down to fall into a pit where their bodies were burned. Uday and Qusay Hussein, the MPs now running the prison have learned, often presided over the executions and liked to operate the gallows themselves. Sometimes they even entered the holding cells to shoot prisoners when the hangings fell behind schedule.

One company of the 504th's soldiers are long-term residents at Abu Ghuraib themselves—they secure the region surrounding the prison. One week before I visited, President Bush, as a gesture of good will, released five hundred of Abu Ghuraib's "least dangerous" prisoners. Apparently these prisoners weren't entirely *non*-dangerous, though. Soldiers told me that the amnesty was followed by an immediate spike in mortar attacks on the prison, as the parolees apparently offered up information on the facility's layout—or launched attacks themselves. The soldiers' own quarters took numerous hits, pulverizing the roof tiles, but fortunately no rounds penetrated the heavy concrete over their living area.

LOTS OF FIGHTING LEFT

The brain trust of the 1-504 gathers every evening for a Battle Update Brief that summarizes the events of the last 24 hours and lays plans for the future. These require

"Secret" security clearance, but here, as in many of my other travels with the 82nd, the battalion commander accords me the privilege of sitting in. This night's proceedings provide clear evidence that there is still much fighting to be done. Within the last day alone, the area experienced a mortar attack and two IED incidents—and explosions thought to be 122mm rockets launched from nine miles away.

How is it known where the rockets came from? Courtesy of the powerful new Q36 and Q37 radar systems, which lay down a thick blanket of radar extending for many miles in every direction. Any time something flies upward through this blanket and comes down somewhere else, the system captures the entry and exit points and the land impact point, calculates the trajectory backwards, and almost instantly yields the coordinates of the launch site.

A response can be dispatched with a single radio call. Should soldiers be patrolling near the firing point, they will chase the shooters down. Otherwise, the coordinates are sent to U.S. counterfire batteries—a mortar or an artillery team kept on station at all times. Within minutes, they rain fire down on the Iraqi attackers. That takes all the fun out of launching an assault on an American position.

The Iraqis have figured out ways to reduce their chances of getting punished, however. They "shoot and scoot"—popping off a handful of rounds, sometimes from the back of a truck, and then hightail it out of there. Other times they'll launch assaults from places where they know American decency will offer some protection—from amidst a residential neighborhood, say, or from alongside a busy highway. Before the counterfire batteries are let loose, soldiers check their maps to see what's located at the coordinates given to them by the Q36. If there's a significant chance of hurting innocent people, the shelling is cancelled.

Insurgent rockets can be particularly hard to respond to. For one thing, they can be launched from farther away than a mortar. And because they fly horizontally rather than looping steeply upward and then down, they sometimes evade radar detection. Of course, rockets require careful aiming, and the improvised launching systems the Iraqis have had to resort to have not been very precise. They are improving, though.

"These latest rockets landed just outside the walls of our camp," warns battalion commander Marshall Hagen. "I want you to watch out. These guys know what they're doing."

■ ■

The battalion intelligence officer's summary of the latest classified information also makes clear that there remain plenty of threats in—or on their way to—this theater. Intercepted information reveals that al-Qaeda is endeavoring to orchestrate large-scale car-bomb attacks against Coalition forces and Iraqi targets over the next month. Various operatives of a cell (believed to be working out of Mosul) have been overheard discussing the purchase of forty vehicles in Syria for conversion into car bombs. (A string of violent car-bomb blasts does indeed take place in the weeks after this warning goes out.)

We also learn that terrorists are moving more sophisticated surface-to-air missiles into the environs of Baghdad International Airport. They would like to down a plane and so discourage Royal Jordanian Airlines from resuming commercial flights to the airport, as is being considered.

There is discussion of a grenade attack that injured some members of the local city council when they met a few days ago. One of the victims was a woman who had criticized the Americans for detaining local Iraqis. She stopped complaining after that, reports an officer.

Lieutenant Colonel Hagen is informed that one of the Iraqi interpreters employed at this camp has been discovered to be working for, and possibly related to, an important wanted insurgent. The translator will be arrested tomorrow. Hagen then reminds his officers to avoid divulging information on tactics to interpreters, not to tell them where a raiding mission is headed until they are on their way in the vehicle, and to keep an ear cocked for hints of false translations or other duplicity.

In general, the numerous Iraqi interpreters now working for the Coalition have been trustworthy and effective—a great many have even become important sources of intelligence, cultural information and character assessment on detainees. Quite a few of them are college students (I became acquainted with computer science, English literature and art majors), women, religious or ethnic minorities, or others estranged from the fallen regime, and they often show their pleasure that Iraq is being pushed onto a new course.

Their work takes courage; they don't live at the U.S. camps, but go home to Iraqi neighborhoods each night, and more than twenty-five translators working for the Coalition have died, many of them assassinated. "I've very much come to admire some of the interpreters, who've displayed great nerve in trying to help their country," Lieutenant Colonel Dave Haight tells me. "I was always professionally committed to this mission, but as I've become friendly with translators, and certain contractors and local residents, I've also become *personally* very committed to building a new, healthier Iraq. I would really like to leave these people a less cruel world to live in."

When I ask Major Stock whether he worries about spies being planted among his translators, he suggests that insurgents plotting such a course would do well to worry about the obverse. "It works both ways—when they see how we treat people, what our goals are for their country, how Americans work, many of them shift their loyalties very dramatically in the direction of the Coalition." But any single spy could do damage, so care is exercised in how Iraqi-national linguists are employed. The same precautions are observed when Iraqi police or Iraqi Civil Defense Corps soldiers are brought in on an operation. Destinations are withheld until the last moment, and outside communication is cut off in the period between combat briefings and the commencement of action.

In a sneaky guerilla war there can be no complacency. Despite the many threats they face, though, the officers are remarkably calm, intrepid, and often even cheerful. Lieutenant Colonel Hagen runs a brisk meeting, interjecting pointed comments and questions, firing off queries and instructions, striding through reports from the field like he strides across the plains of central Iraq during a mission—with the long, rapid gait of a lean and rangy 6'4" athlete.

Amidst an operation, Hagen likes to roam quickly from point to point to stay right on top of the action, and he is as quiet as he is speedy. As I shadow him for two days, I find I need to keep a close watch, else he will have slipped off to observe some new thing while I've been busy taking pictures or listening in on an interrogation. Fortunately, we happen to be a threesome: the commander who will be leading the Marines when they take over this sector in a couple of months is visiting this week, so I have two human landmarks to navigate by as we glide among soldiers and vehicles, through the farmhouses and sheep and goats and scrub palms of rural Iraq.

It's a small world. The incoming Marine commander, Lieutenant Colonel Brennan Byrne, turns out to be a subscriber to *The American Enterprise,* the magazine I edit. Byrne is a naturally buoyant redhead, and he has arrived here full of energy, confidence and enthusiasm. He reports that his 1st Division grunts, who did heavy fighting in Iraq last year before rotating out, are itching to come back and do their part in pushing the country further down the road toward stability and peace.

Like his commanding officer, Marine General James Mattis, Byrne plans to put great emphasis on earning the good will of ordinary Iraqis. He smiles and waves at villagers and lights up the faces of local kids by showing them digital photos he's snapped. One of the reasons for rotating troops is to bring in fresh ideas and renewed eagerness, so Byrne's zest will come in handy.

Byrne and his men have got their work cut out for them, though. At one farmhouse a knot of young children happily receive his handshakes and a new soccer ball. But as we leave, I notice that right in front of that same house there are three craters left by roadside bombs intended for Americans. It would be nearly impossible to plant a bomb there without the knowledge of the family we've just been smiling with.

And I remember that not so long ago, some soldiers of this battalion had a grenade thrown at them by an Iraqi boy very much like those who received this morning's gifts. The perpetrator was nine years old.

NEW BLOOD

When I left for this latest visit to Iraq at the beginning of 2004, the American press was full of pessimistic speculation about what would happen when, over a period of about ninety days, nearly all of the combat-hardened troops in the country would be pulled out and replacements brought in. I was a little concerned myself about the loss of institutional memory and street savvy that might result. But watching the actual transition take place in Baghdad and in the Sunni Triangle around Fallujah made me relax.

For one thing, contrary to some alarmist reporting about clueless, pot-bellied National Guard units taking over, most of the troops being brought in are not newbies. In fact, many of those being inserted into the toughest locales are themselves very recent combat veterans. The brigade of the 82nd Airborne rotating out of Baghdad was replaced by another brigade of the 82nd that had only recently returned from service under fire in Afghanistan. There are certainly important things the newcomers will need to learn about the neighborhood, but they're already quite familiar with Islamic culture, and experienced in countering terror warfare amongst a civilian population.

Likewise with the 1st Marine Division that moved into the Fallujah area. This is the same unit that fought its way up through the country early in 2003, then went home at the end of the spring. For a large majority of the Marines, this is their second Iraq tour in less than eighteen months, so their learning curve is obviously short.

A second reason not to panic about Iraq troop rotations is that the handoffs are being done in a very thorough way. The replacement commanders arrive in the country and start picking the brains of their predecessors weeks or months before they assume responsibility. Their subordinate officers also come over and meet their counterparts, get briefed on who's who in each neighborhood, watch the sifting of intelligence and sit in on active war councils. The Army likes to conduct "left seat, right seat" operations, where the outgoing and incoming peers ride side by side during missions, then eventually switch seats physically as the command authority transfers. In the process, a considerable amount of nitty-gritty operational know-how is transferred.

This is vastly more than the troops now finishing up in Iraq were given when they arrived. "At my handoff in August of 2003, I got nothing but a 'See ya!,' quite literally," says battalion commander Hagen. "I arrived, and five days later they were gone." The first relief troops had to invent and improvise as they went along. Platoon commander Andrew Blickhahn of the 325th, for instance, explains that "we weren't very good at intelligence when we first got here. But we've gotten quite good. And most of the lessons we've learned will now transfer easily."

When new units arrive, voluminous briefing books, maps, operating procedures, patrol routes—you name it—are handed over lock, stock and barrel. A set of fully functioning bases is also transferred, in which vital preparations like security walls, food services and blast-resistant barracks have largely been completed. It's also an enormous advantage that the local advisory councils, the Iraqi police, the Iraqi Civil Defense Corps and other institutions have already been (arduously) put together, and are now beginning to operate with some momentum. All this can be inherited.

A third reason not to fear troop changeovers is that after a year, a fresh set of eyeballs and a reinvigorated level of enthusiasm can be quite useful. "I would estimate that our combat effectiveness peaked around our sixth month," says Lieutenant Michael Eitelman of the Baghdad-based 325th. "After a while you get tired, and worn down a little bit psychologically. You get accustomed to your surroundings. You let your guard down. You stop thinking of new ideas." The extra energy and problem-solving perspective of the replacement troops may be expected to counterbalance most of their greenhorn mistakes.

BALANCING THE HARD AND THE SOFT

As they prepared during the winter to leave for their March Iraq mission, some of the incoming Marine officers made splashy statements to the press about how differently they were going to do things compared with U.S. Army practices. They promised a softer, friendlier approach that would win more Iraqi cooperation. They talked about going into the streets without helmets or body armor in order to present a gentler face; and they considered a different color of combat fatigues so Iraqis would know the U.S. Army was gone and a new bunch was in control. The Army, having slogged pretty impressively through a difficult year, took all this as an implicit criticism—and it was not much appreciated.

There is absolutely no question that efforts to woo neutral Iraqis are critical to pacifying the country, so it was wise for the Marines to head into their job making this a priority. Under the strain of daily attacks, it's understandable that America's fighting Joes might become suspicious and curt with Iraqis, so it's essential to keep reminding them that everyday citizens must be treated differently from the fanatically hostile splinter groups that are on the attack. Otherwise, Iraq's potentially sensible middle could end up disinclined to cooperate with Coalition efforts. For that very reason, the U.S. Army has carried out elaborate community work and made great efforts to cultivate local allies and speed the resuscitation of Iraqi society.

Yet caution and good sense are needed. "It's great to be nice. But we've found that if you let up for one second against the bad guys, they're right back at your throat," warns Lieutenant Colonel Brian Drinkwine. As one Army officer says, "Shaking hands and handing out presents is easy until about the third IED tears up your men. Then you shift to the position we're in now: wanting to make friends, but not having any illusion that the missing element is warmth from our side. The reality is that there is a hardcore minority here who cannot be won over by any reasonable effort; they can only be incapacitated. Until then I could never encourage my soldiers to let down their guard."

Moreover, there is a time and a place for everything. In vast stretches of Iraq, the population is predominantly neutral or friendly to the Coalition forces that have toppled the old regime. And in such places, soldiers can indeed appear without body armor, presenting a more relaxed public face. But in severely recalcitrant towns like Fallujah, passing out candy can be more than fruitless: it can be deadly. American naiveté sometimes assumes that all other people operate in good faith, just as we try to. But there are deeply irrational, blood-feuding groups that simply will not meet a negotiator halfway. There are regimes and cultures that must be broken and forcibly modified: Nazism, Japanese feudalism, the Cosa Nostra, Latin American oligarchies, drug lords, Islamic fundamentalists, other extremists.

In most parts of Iraq, and for the vast proportion of Iraqis, the gentle approach is surely the correct one. But in a few dark holes, the necessary prescription is hard warfare: destruction or detention of the enemy, and those who shelter the enemy. In my travels across very different parts of Iraq, I have seen the need for both styles of policing.

Army General David Petraeus of the 101st Airborne actually put into place a regimen almost exactly like what the Marines are now proposing for the Sunni Triangle. He mounted signs throughout his men's command posts and barracks reading "What have you done today to win Iraqi hearts and minds?" In the relatively calm northern districts that Petraeus administered, this was probably the correct strategy, and it succeeded in many ways. But his region flared into violence on several occasions toward the end of his shift, and I am told by people who have studied the north closely that there is reason to think General Petraeus's comparative gentleness with, for instance, ex-Baathists in Mosul had something to do with their revived audacity in late 2003.

There is a fine line to be walked here. This can be operationally tricky, and psychologically difficult for the soldiers. Tragically, one of the soldiers killed in Fallujah, where I write this, died when he was ambushed while trying to do good—he was on his way to donate classroom supplies to a local school.

Similarly, only a few minutes after giving Fallujans a historic gift—their first open city council vote—soldiers of the 505th Regiment were attacked with a street bomb. Many of the GIs here have been bombed or shot at on multiple occasions. If they don't much feel like playing soccer with Fallujans these days, who can blame them?

As he reflected on the nine months he and his soldiers had spent in Baghdad, Colonel Kurt Fuller noted that this was the very first time in history when U.S. forces have participated in large-scale urban fighting while simultaneously rebuilding the area being contested. While they were conducting more than 500 raids, searching at least

25,000 houses and capturing more than 2,200 suspected insurgents, the paratroopers also set in motion $17 million worth of building projects, repaired 320 schools and 24 medical clinics, and established 15 democracy councils across the city. While rebuilding markets and fixing roads, his men endured 130 firefights, 39 mortar attacks, 25 ambushes, 41 RPG assaults and 140 roadside bombings.

Fuller commended his troopers for demonstrating an ability to accomplish both of their missions. "These soldiers treated Iraqis with dignity and respect unless they were given reason not to—and they only killed when it was absolutely necessary. They proved to the people of this community through their honorable behavior and iron discipline that we are who we say we are, that our reason for being here is both noble and just, that we are here to heal, not to hurt, and to liberate, not to occupy."

There are those who have suggested the U.S. Army should be reconfigured into two different kinds of forces: one that fights lightning wars with great efficiency and violence, and a constabulary force that administers the peace after the war. This suggestion sounds much more plausible on paper than it does amidst the realities of Iraq.

"I'd like to know which kind of force that theory would prescribe for Iraq today," responds Lieutenant Colonel John Castles, the quiet, thoughtful commander of about a thousand of the 82nd's paratroopers in Baghdad, when I ask him about this. "Hardly a day passes where we don't need to both fight and build up something here. And each wing needs the other to succeed."

Commander Drinkwine has concluded much the same thing from his time battling the insurgency in Fallujah.

He tells his soldiers they must have "a day face and a night face." That is, there are times they need to be open and friendly, and times when they must strike very hard. Sometimes they must do each of these things one right after another. But they must struggle to keep their actions and their feelings compartmentalized, and appropriately matched to whichever group of Iraqis they are dealing with.

Drinkwine also urges his men to "make sure that our video exceeds our audio." In other words, the soldiers must *demonstrate* respect, dignity, tolerance and accountability, not just preach these qualities. They must show Iraqis peaceful justice, even while serving as the tough sheriffs on a violent frontier.

Once again we see the importance of delicately balancing the hard and the soft in the prosecution of this guerilla war. And yet again we see how much this complex campaign against terror demands of our military men and women.

AVOIDING DEPENDENCY

In one place where I thought the Army might be making a counterinsurgency mistake—their consolidation of bases in Baghdad—I'm now not so sure.

In the southwestern quadrant of Baghdad alone, controlled by the 82nd Airborne, there were fourteen different U.S. bases. The classic military literature on how to fight a guerilla war says that this is exactly the right strategy. Counterinsurgency fighters must avoid isolated fortresses and get out among the populace, where they can make friends and disarm enemies, gather intelligence and be positioned to intervene quickly.

But in late 2003 and early 2004, most of those Army posts scattered throughout Baghdad were closed down. Nearly all the troopers of the 82nd were consolidated into a very large property, surrounded by a brand-new fifteen-foot wall, in a former industrial area south of the city. This makes it easier to provision the soldiers, and with only one perimeter to be guarded instead of many, they are probably safer. But they are also cut off from the neighborhoods. Intelligence doesn't flow in as easily, and observations that used to be made right outside the gate now happen only if a long patrol is dispatched. And responses to incidents are less rapid.

By most counterinsurgency theory, this is the wrong way to go. "I'm against it," one company commander tells me. "We've got a concrete wall around us and a three-hour wait for walk-ins to get access to an American. When we were in our neighborhood base I used to have a line outside the entrance, and I got tons of useful information that way every single day. Since we moved in here, the amount of information I have to work with has plummeted."

But there is another side to the story. This consolidation was not undertaken for the convenience or security of the American troops. It was ordered by Baghdad-area commander General Martin Dempsey, I discovered, for very specific operational reasons. His directive ordering the relocations states that by pulling American troops out of the city's heart and resettling them at a few perimeter points, he expects to 1) remove a psychological irritant in the neighborhoods by sharply diminishing the appearance that this is an occupying army, and 2) make Iraqis take more responsibility for their own security, rather than let them become entirely dependent on American protection.

Lieutenant Colonel Castles gives his own explanation: "My battalion alone had five different operating bases at one point, and that was the right answer when we first arrived, because there was not much structure or law enforcement in this country. But as we've started showing progress in the city, I've felt it was important to gradually pull back and let the Iraqis run their own business. And this has basically worked.

"The biggest challenge is intel—getting people to come up to us at this new base as they did at the old ones. There was definitely a dip when we moved. But now that we've settled here and people are finding us, our contacts are rising again. I'm confident we can keep ourselves open enough to maintain the flow of public feedback."

Colonel Fuller, who has had more combat experience in small wars amidst civilian populations than almost any other officer in the U.S. Army (Grenada, Panama, Kuwait, Haiti, Kosovo and now the second Iraq war), offers a comparison when I ask him about the wisdom of the base consolidation. "In Kosovo, we have gotten ourselves trapped in scores of scattered camps. We stayed too long and now can't withdraw because we're the only stabilizers and preventers of violence.

"We went into Kosovo in June of 1994—a long time ago. And despite better infrastructure there, and friendlier people, and the lack of any insurgency like we're fighting here, we are nowhere near being able to pull out. We're stuck.

"I consolidated our operating bases to avoid creating that same dependency among the people of Baghdad. We have to turn things over to them. Even if they're initially not up to the full responsibility. The way you learn how to provide security is by just doing it.

"You know, you can very quickly create a welfare state where everyone relies completely upon the occupying force to solve their problems. The key piece of this fight is to get the good Iraqis to take it over for themselves. We're pulling back to get operational standoff. And to avoid generating dependency on us among the residents of this city."

The Baghdad base consolidation, I've concluded, is perhaps foremost a sign of the confidence our military feels that they've gotten the guerila war under control. "One of the reasons for the intelligence dip we saw in the late fall around here was not our November move, but simply that we'd already picked up so many of the main troublemakers," says Dave Elsen, 3rd Battalion's military intelligence officer.

The arrival of the Marines will bring yet another take on this question. General Mattis has pushed his commanders to study a Vietnam-era program that spread U.S. platoons into villages and communities where, as local residents, they were able to pacify the immediate region while collecting information and developing local allegiances that helped the wider prosecution of the war. The Marines are giving special "community policing" and language training to one platoon from each of the nine battalions they are bringing into Iraq this spring. The intention is to place these so-called "CAP" units in some critical locale where they can chip away at insurgents from within the neighborhood. Lieutenant Colonel Byrne tells me he is thinking about posting one of his platoons in an Iraqi police station in some area where they feel particularly under siege. Time will tell, but local experiments and trial-and-error tests of this sort are the best ways to find effective paths in a low-intensity fight like this one.

8

HERE WE COME

Our military leaders in Iraq are edging toward the next stage—when the Iraqi police and army will increasingly take control of their own security, while American forces serve as a backstop. This is progress. Completing the process will require patience, though, and in the meantime, experience has taught U.S. troops the importance of taking the fight to the guerillas.

At 0500 this morning, the Red Devils kick off their latest initiative, an all-day operation called Desert Swarm. For more than an hour, our convoy of open trucks roars along the cross-country highways, the icy wind slicing through our thin clothing, leaving us shivering violently and huddling together for a bit of warmth. This raid will bring about five hundred troopers into the town of Uwaylim, source of numerous recent attacks. In recent weeks, Americans have hardly touched this zone. This is a tactic that commanders use to lull insurgents: they stay away from a sector long enough to make local troublemakers feel safe, at which point the rebels begin stashing weapons and hiding wanted men in the area. Then, when the time is ripe, the 82nd swoops in and scoops out whatever is to be found.

Soldiers have taken serious fire from Uwaylim. A local radical mosque is suspected to be fomenting attacks. Several desperados are thought to have recently taken up refuge in the town. Almost certainly there are IEDs planted along local roads, waiting for the right moment to be detonated.

Literally walking through a large "sand table" map of the region laid out in paint, rope and wooden blocks on a 40' x 40' expanse of bare dirt at one edge of the camp, commanders rehearse the raid. Various types of possible resistance are discussed. The most difficult part, warns Lieutenant Colonel Hagen, could be getting out. "There are only a handful of outlet roads from the area, and they'll have five or six hours to set up IEDs and ambushes along them while we're conducting our searches in the central zone. So take great care."

One reason this area has prickled with attacks is because it was the final location of a major Republican Guard unit at the end of the hot war. The unit left behind voluminous ammo stashes in the groves and along the canals and roads, giving local miscreants much to work with. There are indications that many of the male residents were soldiers themselves—old helmets, empty ammo boxes, optical sights and shell casings litter many of the yards and homes. In one house where I accompany searchers, a pair of night-vision goggles is found. Parked in yards and driveways are even several tanks (engines, sights and other valuable parts stripped out months ago)—

looking like the Iraqi version of an Appalachian pickup truck up on cement blocks, stowed away because you never know when it's going to come in handy.

Soldiers passing through this quadrant have been shot at recently, in some cases in sophisticated coordinated ambushes using a combination of IEDs, machine guns and small arms. This suggests to American officers they may have brushed up against a security zone for something or someone the insurgents want to protect. Maybe a large cache? A cell leader?

As the sun begins to rise, I follow the battalion commander past a mosque and a weedy canal to a collection of buildings where two brothers on this morning's target list, Mohammed and Jassim Khudari, are rumored to live. Two of the homes are grubby farm houses with the usual complement of a few cows, some chickens, a pigeon roost. The other is more pretentious. As dawn blooms, a squad rouses a large, hard-faced man from the main house, who admits right away that he is Jassim. A search quickly yields multiple ID cards with the same picture but a variety of names. There are also documents that indicate Jassim was a major in the Iraqi army and a member of Saddam's Presidential Security Service.

"These guys are real bad about keeping their souvenirs from the former regime," chuckles an intelligence officer, as he pulls out a letter that begins, "Our love for Saddam Hussein is deep in our hearts. . . ." In the house next door, number-two brother Mohammed is captured without a struggle, and a collection of videotapes showing Chechen Islamic guerillas killing Russians (a favorite among Muslim jihadists) is found. Most damning, the main house contains a wireless phone with two handsets and a large supplemental antenna jury-rigged to the base unit.

Since there are no phone lines to plug into in most of Iraq, there is only one use for such a device: setting off IEDs. Fighters wire the relay inside the phone to a blasting cap attached to artillery shells. Then they dial the phone number programmed into the base unit, and when it rings—boom! The combat engineer in this Army squad, an expert on the insurgents' electronic innovations, has seen this particular phone model used many times in IED attacks. Other favorite gadgets used for remote detonating are garage door openers and car alarms.

The paratroopers of the 504th know all about the dangers of IEDs. They have named the just-opened Internet-access tent at their base after Captain Ernesto Blanco, a Texas A&M grad and support platoon officer known as "Big Ern," who was killed when his convoy was bombed in nearby Karmah on December 28. Many or most of the troopers I am with have had a close, personal brush with a roadside explosion; some squads have been bombed three or four times.

All told, each of the battalions I visited in Iraq in January had lost a half-dozen or more men. "After ambushes or mortar attacks, sometimes we just have to get out a hose to wash away the blood left in the bay," one medevac helicopter pilot told me quietly.

And then there are the non-life-threatening risks and strains that soldiers bear. Many of the paratroopers in the 82nd served the better part of a year in Afghanistan, were home for seven months, and then redeployed to Iraq. They know the reason they've been sent into the very angriest portion of the country is because they are some of the best soldiers in our military. They are proud of that, and amazingly spirited, energetic and uncomplaining in their day-to-day work. But there are many pressures on them.

"When I get home in May I will have spent two of the previous twenty-eight months with my eight- and four-year-old kids," says Captain Gary Love.

"Yeah, and Captain Ryan Huston has spent the last four Christmases away from home," someone else chimes in.

"Over the last eighteen months, I've been deployed overseas 446 days. And counting," says Captain Chris Cirino with a big smile. "But I'm not complaining. I'm a professional soldier, and I find this life very satisfying. On some levels I even like being over here."

RAIDING THE RAIDERS

Back in the field with the soldiers of the 504th, the radio crackles to report that other individuals targeted in this morning's raid have been picked up. That puts the battalion at four for four in captures this morning. At every house they enter, the paratroopers do a visual weapons search and use mine detectors to probe outdoor areas for metallic stashes. Officers diligently question male residents, catching many in lies or improbable stories, which they then try to leverage into information on anti-Coalition forces in the area.

Hagen stops at a secretive signals-intelligence truck with an antenna that I am not allowed to photograph.

The operator is able to monitor some neighborhood conversations as soldiers pull up outside various houses, and he passes along tidbits he has gleaned to the commander. Next we sweep over to a home where a cooperative farmer reports that some brothers living across the road behind some date palms were the masterminds of a bombing and fierce ambush against American soldiers on November 7. "Yeah, those were our guys who got hit," says Hagen, noticeably perking up his ears at this information. In that heavy firefight, two of his men earned decorations for valor.

"It'd be nice to get some payback for that one, sir," declares a soldier.

"You know, the platoon that got hit then, the 1st, is here today," comments a sergeant. "Including Sergeant Ferguson, who can't hear any more since the attack."

"I'd sure like to see a good firefight initiated by us, for once," the sergeant adds.

The Iraqi informant speaks up again. The same brothers who set up the ambush also recently murdered a local man after he gave information to the Americans.

"Don't worry, we'll keep your identity from being known. And we won't go directly there from here. So they won't be able to associate you with our arrival," reassures the soldier doing the questioning.

At this moment a small pickup truck creeps down the dirt trail we are standing next to. Two men in front gesticulate excitedly. Sitting upright in the truck bed is a very sour, very swollen woman. "Beeeby, Beeby!" I hear the men say as they bump by on their way to a midwife, or hospital, or whoever assists in this place when new lives begin.

It's sometimes hard to remember that the normal dramas of life continue to unfold throughout this war zone: families forming, students studying for exams, boys wooing girls. On several tense combat patrols in the heart of Iraqi cities, I've been startled by automatic weapons fire outside a mosque, only to realize that it's not an attack, but a wedding celebration. (A strange custom, I must say, and more than a little dangerous in these conditions.)

We cross into the back field of the farmer-informant, where a knot of soldiers has gathered. An alert private, noticing a heap of earth in a strange place in a shallow irrigation channel, has uncovered two plastic bags full of AK-47 ammunition and clips. The plot thickens. "Where did these come from?" queries a squad leader.

"I don't know. Maybe our neighbor planted them there," answers the farmer's son.

"That's not possible so close to your house. You have a loud dog."

"It's been cold. The dog must have stayed in his hole."

"I think you're lying."

The friendly informant's family has suddenly turned out to possess an impermissibly large quantity of arms. Are they insurgents themselves? Or have they stocked up to protect themselves from vengeful neighbors? Who can be trusted?

Hagen decides to let the evidence sort this situation out. He gets on the radio to his operations officer and they plan a quick raid on the houses of the two brothers across the road. An hour and a half later, their farmsteads are surrounded by Bradley fighting vehicles and perhaps forty dismounted Americans. Soldiers enter the premises and begin to question the wives and older men of the clan. The brothers, they are told, are "at work."

"Where?"

"We don't know."

Very likely the two men are skittering along some nearby ditch or through a palm grove as we speak. But the soldiers now know where they live, and they will very soon return, probably in the middle of the night, repeatedly if necessary, until they have questioned the men or driven them from the area.

DREAMLAND

I've now shifted to another of the 82nd's battalions, the 1-505, which is responsible for Fallujah city proper. In a country that could yield a regular highlights film of urban snake pits, this is one of the most troublous assignments in Iraq. Over the last few months, this battalion has been running more combat operations than any other unit in Iraq, averaging a major raid about every eighteen hours, and occasionally executing as many as five separate hits in a single day. Having been assigned to Iraq's worst hornet's nest, they have access to almost every resource the U.S. Army can provide: a full squadron of Kiowa reconnaissance helicopters, a borrowed set of M-1 tanks and Bradleys on call, an extra company of riflemen from the 10th Mountain Division and a gaggle of secretive Special Forces operators.

"The very best Special Forces units in the world are here," Lieutenant Colonel Brian Drinkwine reminds his men at his nightly commander's briefing. "Every special operator in America wants to come work with you."

I don't ask who exactly the bearded guys in civilian clothes and Japanese vehicles running around camp are— Green Berets? Delta Force?—but clearly they are very active. They sneak into the city on motorcycles, bikes and domestic vehicles, and provide names and addresses of lots of bad guys at every morning's targeting meeting. "All I can say is that things have definitely gotten better since they arrived," states one soldier.

The 1-505's camp has been dubbed Volturno, after a World War II battle in Italy where this unit distinguished itself. The property they have occupied used to be another of the many playpens of Uday Hussein. The dictator's son called it "Dreamland," and spared no expense in emulating the Hollywood look. A vast artificial lake, serving absolutely no purpose but show, was carved into the middle of the desert and filled with water pumped from the miles-distant Euphrates. Pomegranate orchards and desert trees were thickly laid in, and the usual gaudy Baathist residences were erected.

The place is attractive by day, but a little ghostly on the windy, rainy nights we've been having. Between the abandoned skeletons of the palaces (demolished by the Air Force last spring in its attempt to decapitate the Hussein family), the fish flipping in the half-drained lake, the blacked-out military vehicles that suddenly whisk past without warning when the breeze is blowing their engine noise away from you, and thoughts of the depraved bacchanals that must have occurred here, it is a setting ripe for the imagination.

And not really safe: we take mortar fire nearly every day I am here.

I'm staying off on one corner of the property, in a small, cold building with a leaking roof that is squeezed between the ten-foot inner and outer walls that ring the spread, which covers many hundreds of acres. I'm with the scouts and snipers. These are men who slip into forward positions to probe enemy lines and conduct reconnaissance. The snipers carry special .50 caliber and 7.62mm long-barrel rifles topped by very fine scopes, including some designed for night shooting. Recently they have acquired several silencers, one courtesy of the Special Forces, that reduce their weapons' report to that of a pellet gun; so far, they've used these mostly to eliminate dogs whose aggressive yapping threatens to expose their scouting missions.

Hanging in the "hooch" where I'm bunked is one of the snipers' ghillie suits—a shaggy, camouflaged, knee-length cover that makes the wearer disappear into the desert scrub. "I've had that on and laid still around dusk and had hajis walk by so close I could have reached out and grabbed their ankles," says Sergeant Patrick McGuire, using the soldiers' slang for Iraqi nationals, "yet they never noticed me."

The generator used by this group of soldiers threw a piston a few days ago, so we have only a little power rerouted from another generator via an extension cord. It's enough to charge my laptop, thankfully, but the only illumination in the damp, windowless concrete shed I'm occupying is supplied by a string of Christmas lights. So every night for most of a week, when it's time for me to translate my day's accumulation of quick-scrawled paper notes into a computer-written storyline, I must pull the holiday decorations down around my shoulders and, squinting and bobbing my head, decipher enough hand-writing to compose a few paragraphs. Then more dim groping for papers and more clicking at the keys, well into the wee hours. Luckily I learned to touch-type in seventh grade (the most useful class I took in secondary school, next to auto shop), so I don't need to see the keyboard.

It's not exactly Abe Lincoln reading the Bible by fire-light, but it feels a lot like that.

IN THE SNAKE PIT

This battalion is led by something of an odd couple: Lieu-tenant Colonel Drinkwine is a mild, pleasant, reflective man, a northern New Yorker who falls on the intellectual side of the commander spectrum. Operations chief Michael Bottiglieri, a Texan, is both physically and emotionally darker: no-nonsense, a bit curt, secretive, energetic. The two make an effective team.

When they arrived in Fallujah in early September, they encountered many enemies. For one thing, there were huge gangs of looters and criminal elements in the city. In addition to garden-variety domestic felonies, these gangsters were easily recruited by the city's political or religious insurgents as triggermen for guerilla attacks. "There is a whole, detailed tariff here: so many dollars for shooting an RPG at Americans; so many for planting an IED; this much for an IED that makes headline news—

fees ranging to hundreds and thousands of dollars. Executing attacks was a moneymaking business when we arrived here, carried out by penniless people not for principled reasons but for the pay," explains Major Bottiglieri.

There were also the usual ethnic hatreds and clan rivalries that are common throughout Iraq. And personal and family vendettas can sometimes ignite into street anarchy. Once this fall, a group attacked an American patrol, then melted into the neighborhood of an opposing tribe—with the specific hope of provoking the soldiers into attacking the homes of their traditional enemies.

In addition to these troublemakers, the U.S. military had to deal with violent defenders of the previous government, furious over their loss of status. This is a nearly 100 percent Sunni city that has long been one of the most pro-Saddam and pro-Baath places in Iraq. Many officers and soldiers of the Iraqi security forces came from here, and returned here when the old regime dissolved. There is a large neighborhood called the Martyr's District where thousands of widows and orphans were sent to live after losing their household breadwinner in the casualty-heavy Iran-Iraq War. (Having tasted the fruits of Saddam's military incompetence and recklessness, it's not surprising that this is the most Coalition-friendly part of town.)

There are also significant numbers of Islamic fanatics in Fallujah. This is known as the City of Mosques for good reason: there are more than a hundred here, a higher number per capita than in any other part of the country, many of them Wahhabi. Some of the mosques are known hotspots for violence. When open battles broke out in mid-April 2004, the Marines who replaced the 82nd Airborne had to attack several mosques from which they were taking fire.

WALKING FALLUJAH

The same day I arrive, the 505th gets a visit from the in-laws. The 82nd's commanding general Charles Swannack stops by to see how things are proceeding in Iraq's Dodge City, bringing with him the Army officer in charge of the entire country, three-star general Ricardo Sanchez. There is an unusual spread of food and drinks on the picnic table behind the battalion command post, and overhead the F-15s veer so low we can feel the sound waves on our temples as well as in our ears, and see shiny vapor trails frittering off their wings in the early morning damp. A set of Apache attack helicopters adds to the overkill. Surely neon lights are now flashing in the local guerillas' lairs: "Someone worth assassinating has just come to town!"

So General Sanchez has a bristling escort for his walk right down Fallujah's main boulevard. Our convoy of perhaps two dozen vehicles disgorges more than a hundred soldiers into a lot next to what used to be the mayor's office. Two days after Saddam was captured, a protest was organized in front of this facility; it soon grew violent, turning into an all-out attack on the building, the interim city administration, and the Iraqi police guarding the premises. RPGs and rifle fire poured into the structure, demolishing most of the interior. By the time U.S. soldiers suppressed the fight, the mayor had been kidnapped. He had to be rescued in an aggressive operation quickly mounted by Charlie Company.

In the open lot next door to the shell of a building left behind by this riot, General Sanchez greets the local commander of the Iraqi Civil Defense Corps, who tells him he needs more radios, cars and heavy weapons. Then the general walks, with a few dozen paratroopers, several blocks to where a platoon is carrying out a weapons search. Inside a ruined structure right next to the city's largest mosque, soldiers have found resistance paraphernalia, including an improvised cylindrical device fabricated to launch rockets, and a bunch of steel pipes likewise cut for use as firing tubes. A company commander explains that they believe this site was used to launch rockets at the mayor's office.

The premises also contain al-Qaeda literature. Sanchez shows an interest in the tracts and hands one to his translator, asking him to read some of the chapter and section headings.

"What al-Qaeda is."

"Al-Qaeda's relationship to the Taliban."

"Who is Osama bin Laden?"

"Why he went to Afghanistan."

"How [Osama bin Laden] sacrificed his fortune in Saudi Arabia for al-Qaeda."

"The glorious explosion at the American Embassy."

"How to expand the jihad movement."

"Coordination between cells."

"The latest confrontations."

Off in the distance there is a burst of AK-47 fire. We continue our foot tour. At the fringes of our file,

Psychological Operations soldiers hand out five different kinds of leaflets to bystanders. They shove them under the gates in front of houses. "Often it's best if they just find it instead of receiving it in public," reports a PsyOps officer.

One handbill warns that persons attacking Coalition forces will be dealt with severely. Another offers a reward for information on vehicle-mounted weapons. A third shows pictures of shoulder-fired surface-to-air missiles and offers a $2,500 payment to anyone turning one in. Colonel Jeff Smith, the 82nd's brigade commander for this region, takes a personal interest when one teenager tells a soldier he has seen such a weapon.

"Where?" the colonel asks. "I will pay you lots of money for such a thing."

Evasion. "Such things are only outside of Fallujah, not here," the boy replies, as a group gathers around. This is an answer I've heard many times in Iraq when a conversation about resistance fighters gets down to brass tacks. Yes, they are here, it is said, but always over the next hill, in the next town, not in this neighborhood. The colonel quietly tells the boy to come see him privately if he has information, and our party moves on.

The Marine general and colonels who will be taking over the Fallujah region in a few months have been walking with us, and one now asks General Sanchez: "How many years do you think we'll be here, sir?"

"Years," Sanchez answers. "The Iraqis now understand that the former regime is not returning, so we've got that under our belts. Our challenge now is making sure the radicals don't take advantage of the frailty of the political process that is going to take place over the next year or two.

"The period between now and the June political hand-over is a danger zone. We've got to be particularly careful with the Shia. They are not experienced in democratic politics and could overplay their hand and make big problems with their insistence on immediate direct elections.

"The best thing we can do right now is make people really believe we're here to help them rather than to kill them."

CAN WE AFFORD IT?

It's understandable that when a general says we're likely to keep some troops in Iraq for "years," Americans might react with something of a sinking feeling. Americans prefer not to become deeply entangled in other countries; we have no interest in running an empire, nor do we want to pay for one. To provision U.S. and Coalition troops in Iraq and Afghanistan, and then rebuild physical facilities, train security forces and launch economic initiatives in those countries, President Bush requested $87 billion in 2004 spending. That's a lot of money.

Senator Tom Harkin (D-Iowa) opposed the President with these words: "This may not be Vietnam, but boy it sure smells like it. And every time I see these bills coming down for the money, it's costing like Vietnam too." That's nice red rhetoric, but factually, the senator is way off. The costs of the Iraq war are nothing like the expenses of Vietnam.

During Vietnam, U.S. military spending consumed around 10 percent of our nation's gross domestic product. During the Korean War we spent around 14 percent of GDP annually to defend our country. And in World War II, defense spending ate up fully 38 percent of our annual output. Compare those figures with today's spending for the war on terror: in 2004, total defense spending will amount to 4 percent of GDP.

The truth is that a good chunk of the $87 billion requested for 2004 would have been spent even if all our troops were back at their home bases. The 120,000 soldiers in Iraq and the several thousand more in Afghanistan are not going to be demobilized after their work is done. They are going to head back to North Carolina, Kansas, Texas, New York, Georgia and elsewhere; there they will draw salaries, fire off rounds at training ranges and put mileage on their vehicles. Sure, they're pulling extra combat pay now, and operating at a higher intensity. But they are also honing themselves into a far better fighting force as they bring the war on terror to our enemies in their own backyards.

A further truth is that some of today's military spending is catch-up for the 1990s, when the administration and Congress slashed the defense budget to its lowest level in three generations, took a holiday on procurement of new equipment, and chopped training hours and supply purchases. In the Balkans, we nearly ran out of cruise missiles and bombs because of 1990s underinvestment. In Iraq today, many of the Humvees, helicopters and airplanes transporting American forces are older than the men guiding them.

In March 2003, I watched an artillery crew of the 82nd Airborne pull 105mm artillery shells out of crates stamped with the date of manufacture: "May 1970." In about one shell out of every three, the 33-year-old powder bags had dry-rotted, spilling the propellant onto the sand and making the rounds useless.

Ironically, some of the people who claimed that our spending in Iraq is unaffordable have simultaneously argued that the current American force in that country is too small to do the job—and indeed, that the entire U.S. Army needs to be expanded in order to police terrorism. (This is, for instance, John Kerry's position). But that would *really* be expensive, and over a much longer haul (personnel are the major expense in our military budget). And I don't believe it's necessary. The 120,000 U.S. service members in Iraq today represent less than 5 percent of our 2.6-million-person armed forces (1.4 million active duty plus 1.2 million reservists). And in addition to those 2.6 million warriors, our defense department employs 700,000 civilians. That's enough bodies and minds to do the job. Even China, the most populous nation in the world, more than four times our size, has a military of only 2.3 million members.

Our dilemma is not that our fighting force is too small, but that it is located in the wrong places. We still have 75,000 soldiers stationed in Germany, waiting for a Soviet tank thrust that is never going to come. We have 25,000 more in Britain and Italy, another leftover of World War II geopolitics. We have 45,000 troops in Japan! And another 37,000 in Korea. Instead of creating new divisions, we need to accelerate the redeployment of American forces to the globe's new trouble spots, a process that began only creepingly with the end of the Cold War.

And we need to give our existing troops better tools. That's why three-quarters of the President's 2004 spending request is dedicated to new Humvees, better body armor, and other equipment and supplies our soldiers need to hunt down terrorists. Less than $20 billion is being used to help rebuild Iraq: $15 billion to fix electrical, water, communications and transport facilities, $5 billion to set up army and police forces.

Those are no mean sums, but they need to be kept in perspective. Consider that we Americans will spend about $37 billion just this year on salty snacks: potato chips, pretzels, peanuts and such. We'll collectively spend $31 billion on candy in 2004. Can we afford to spend $20 billion to stabilize and reform one of the most dangerous parts of the globe? We might better ask whether we can afford *not* to.

THANKS FOR NOTHING

Of course, Americans aren't the only ones who would benefit from a clampdown on Middle Eastern extremism. Many of our wealthy allies have even higher stakes in our success in Iraq—because of their physical proximity to the danger zone, their heavier dependence upon the region's oil, and their own susceptibility to domestic Islamic terrorism (in France, for instance, a restive 10 percent of the population is now Muslim, a proportion heading toward 20 percent over the next generation). So it certainly would be wise, as well as friendly, if our European colleagues in particular contributed to the process of setting Iraq back on its feet, as the down payment on a new Middle East.

On the military front, we'll never see effective help from most of today's European countries. They aren't up to it. Over the last generation, as author Dennis Prager puts it, "Instead of learning to fight evil, they have only learned that fighting is evil." Not only do today's Europeans lack the will to chase bad guys, they've also left themselves without the means. In December 2003, NATO secretary-general Lord George Robertson bemoaned the fact that the European forces in Afghanistan have only three helicopters. After decades of starving their armed forces, the Europeans have nearly surrendered their ability to project power beyond their own borders.

The Europeans could contribute financially, however, and as the globe's richest collection of nations they should. Their excuse for opting out of the spring war was America's inability to slide a U.N. resolution past French, German and Russian objections. But as reconstruction of Iraq began in earnest in the fall of 2003, U.S. leaders acted as model internationalists. First, the United States lined up a U.N. Security Council resolution in which all parties unanimously agreed that more international aid was needed to rectify the damage done by Saddam Hussein. Then a conference involving more than seventy countries was convened in Madrid to raise the funds needed to lift the former outlaw nation back onto its feet. The Bush administration and Congress led by example with their offer of nearly $20 billion in direct assistance to the Iraqi people.

These U.S. efforts to launch Iraq's rebuilding were conducted in the most gentle "multilateral" fashion. All the things the French and Germans are always lecturing America to do—rely more on diplomacy, share more aid, take less independent action—were carried out. So how was this received by our professed allies? In far too many cases, with a turned back.

The most constructive response came from the Japanese, who pledged $1.5 billion to help the Iraqi people onto a new path in 2004, and a total of $5 billion over several years. Britain offered $825 million starting in 2004. Spain promised $300 million over four years. South Korea, which knows something about achieving a national recovery from war with U.S. assistance, made a pledge of $200 million. Canada offered $150 million, Italy $232 million over three years (plus 3,000 troops). Sweden promised $33 million, and Denmark ponied up $50 million in cash, along with 500 soldiers, and trainers for the Iraqi police.

As for our other Western European partners: France announced it would not be contributing at all, and sent only a low-level delegation to Madrid. Russia offered not a kopek. The same with Belgium. Germany coughed up only $50 million.

German development minister Heidemarie Wieczorek-Zeul insisted that Germany "cannot afford" any help for the Iraqis beyond that. She also stated that she was against forgiving Iraq any of the $4.6 billion it owes Germany, though debt forgiveness would not require any budget outlays. That debt, of course, was rung up through trafficking with Saddam Hussein that was highly profitable to German companies, but mostly useless to today's Iraqis.

The European Union pledged a total of $231 million. Recall that the E.U. as a body has 100 million more people than the United States and a larger cumulative economic output. Which makes its offer—1/86th of the U.S. contribution—look quite miserable.

NEW FRIENDS FOR OLD

Aid pledged in Madrid will not be touched by American administrators or troops, but will go into a trust managed by the World Bank, the United Nations and a committee of Iraqis. It will directly benefit Iraq's traumatized people. It could help avert what would be an unmitigated disaster for all civilized peoples—a radical turn by one of the Middle East's most important nations. So there is no reasonable explanation for any Western nation's refusal to help today's Iraqis more substantially, except this: a desire to obstruct American aims in the region.

Certainly this is the view of the Iraqis themselves. When invited to address the U.N. Security Council in December 2003, Iraq's foreign minister criticized European dawdlers for "settling scores with the United States" at the expense of "helping to bring stability to the Iraqi people." Hoshyar Zebari excoriated opponents of Iraq's liberation for their selfish agendas. "One year ago, the Security Council was divided between those who wanted to appease Saddam Hussein and those who wanted to hold him accountable," and as a result it "failed to help rescue the Iraqi people from a murderous tyranny.... Today we are unearthing thousands of victims in horrifying testament to that failure."

To the French and others who cast aspersions on the interim Iraqi government, he answered: "As Iraqis, we strongly disagree with those of you who question the legitimacy of the present Iraqi authorities. I'd like to remind you that the Governing Council is the most representative and democratic governing body in the region. The members of the Security Council should be reaching out and encouraging this nascent democracy in a region well known for its authoritarian rule."

There is good evidence that the failure of the French, Germans, Russians and others to do their part in rescuing Iraq is based on anti-American obstructionism more than sincere differences in foreign-policy aims. Perhaps the simplest proof is Afghanistan. The Afghan war was not controversial with Old Europe: all the allies agreed that the Taliban were a blight on Central Asia, that the al-Qaeda cells sheltered and trained in that country presented a grave danger to the world, and that there was an urgent need to remove both entities militarily, and then rebuild Afghanistan's government and civil society.

Yet our allies, who were glad to have America do the dirty work of rooting the Islamist fundamentalists out of their caves, have not lived up even to their modest promises of financial support in this uncontroversial case—they are way behind on their pledges of aid to repair Afghanistan. According to the British charity Care International, aid to Afghanistan was just $75 per capita in the latest year. That compared with $193 per capita in Rwanda, $326 in Bosnia, $288 in Kosovo, and $195 in East Timor—lands in a comparable state of recovery from war. In a September 2003 conference in Dubai, the U.S. offered an additional $1.2 billion to stabilize Afghanistan, and we hoped our allies would come close to matching that. The European Union, alas, put up about $49 million. At a Berlin conference in April 2004, the Americans pledged yet another billion dollars in help for the Afghans, bringing our total aid to more than $4 billion since 2001. The United States is putting up more Afghan aid this year than all the rest of the world put together. The European Union offered less than $300 million. France and Russia gave nothing.

In his recent book *Anti-Americanism,* the great French writer Jean-François Revel warns that a poisonous antipathy toward the United States has taken deep root in Western Europe. And he cautions that this new animosity will rarely be something the U.S. can correct or negotiate away—because it is a psychological side-effect of America's galloping success. Today's deepest anti-Americanism in Europe and other parts of the world, Revel warns, is built on envy and ideological bile.

The E.U. recently asked Europeans which countries they regard as posing the greatest threat to world peace. In first place, selected by 59 percent of Europeans, was Israel. Second place was a three-way tie: the United States, North Korea and Iran (each picked by 53 percent of respondents). Among the countries that Europeans ranked lower than the U.S. as menaces were Afghanistan, Iraq, Syria, Libya, China and Russia. A different 2003 poll taken in France found that when asked to select "words most suitable to describe" the United States, terms like "violence" (35 percent), "imperialism" (27 percent), "racism" (23 percent) and "inequality" (39 percent) were some of the favorite responses.

The United States must recognize some hard facts about our European Cold War allies: that they will often be obstructionist in the years ahead. Our unsuccessful attempts to shame our European brethren into doing more of their share in lifting up Iraq and Afghanistan make that clear. This suggests the U.S. will need to be steelier about acting without their help in the coming decades. Fortunately, new allies—including many fervent ones like the Eastern Europeans, and emerging friends in places like the Persian Gulf—will rise to make common cause with America as she pursues a foreign policy based on human liberty and an end to terrorism. But we need to understand that our future international partners will often be new ones, frequently from younger, rising nations that are less infirm and reactionary in their foreign policies.

Goodbye to France and Germany. Australia, Poland and democratic Iraq: here we come.

9

WHAT IT TAKES TO WIN

Thursday brings the third meeting of the newly formed Fallujah Provisional Advisory Council. In this city, you don't just call a democratic political meeting to order; you have to bring in a company of heavily armed paratroopers to keep the premises and the participants from being blown up. The Thursday before, ABC newsman Ted Koppel was here to observe this same gathering and got caught in an RPG and automatic-weapons attack launched from the public plaza, often used for protests, which lies right in front of this building.

And so, this morning, eighteen trucks and 116 heavily armed men roll into the city—passing herds of goats grazing on garbage scattered along the streets, Iraqis on the roadside blithely welding metal without eye shields, storefront shops selling bananas, and truck drivers and day laborers clustered in groups waiting for someone to hire them for a little cash.

About an hour before the scheduled event, we clatter into the compound housing the city youth center (or "Uouth Center," as the sign reads), one of the few local halls big

186

enough and defensible enough to house a meeting for forty-two councilors. Snipers climb onto the roofs of several adjoining buildings, Alpha Company foot patrols venture out into the surrounding neighborhoods, gun trucks position themselves facing outward, and explosives experts give the interior of the building a once-over.

Meanwhile, an equally determined search is launched for the youth center's collection of boxing gloves. There is a large, professional-style boxing ring set up, rather incongruously, in the building's courtyard. On previous visits, the soldiers noticed a couple of sets of gloves lying about, and decided that a match or two staged during the quiet hour before the councilors start to arrive would be just the thing to enliven their week. Apart from the natural yearnings of high-spirited and slightly bored young men, there happens to be something of a grudge to be settled between two paratroopers—one of them in the scouts, the other a chaplain's assistant. Everyone agrees that a few rounds in the ring would be a splendid way to resolve their feud, and the soldiers in question are eager to strip off their body armor and spar. Alas, the gloves cannot be located anywhere, and since bare-knuckle brawls are not tolerated in the Army, there will be no entertainment this morning other than that provided by the budding politicians.

Because of the security strains in this region, the local democracy councils are not nearly so far along as in the Baghdad area and some other parts of Iraq. Here, the Army officers still provide the energy and direction, while the locals listen and question.

The interim mayor, a cheerful little bantam rooster with a flashing smile, greets arriving councilors at the door, but he seems a mildly comical figure who lacks weight. In the entry hall he fusses excitedly with a small box of goodies from America someone has given him. "What's this?" he asks, holding up a dispenser of Speed Stick deodorant.

The soldier points to his underarms: "To make you smell nice."

Mayor Ra'ad returns a slightly quizzical look. "And this, for my wife?" he asks, pointing to a can of Gillette shaving cream.

"Not unless she has a beard," says the soldier with a grin.

But the transition to Iraqi self-direction is very much under way. The meeting opens with a nice little speech by the mayor, who states that Iraq's regression over the last generation is the result of thoroughgoing corruption in Iraqi society, from top to bottom. He presents a brief but eloquent plea for greater public rectitude and more concern for the needy, saying that such ethical concerns will be the key to healing the city. Next, a trio of lawyers read their draft of a proposed set of city by-laws. And then the council takes the very first vote of its existence: to choose a council president.

It all has the feeling of a senior class election, with a call for nominations from Lieutenant Colonel Drinkwine, speeches by the candidates on why they are the right man for the job, and finally a vote. But this is no ordinary popularity contest; it is a historic occasion—Fallujah's maiden stab at genuine representative democracy.

Drinkwine passes out blank ballots and explains the concept and practice of a secret vote. He calls a judge, a lawyer and a local imam to the stage to ceremoniously open the completed ballots and read them aloud, one at a time. In the end, a businessman with an engineering degree is selected as the new president of the Fallujah Provisional Advisory Council, immediately taking his place on the stage with the American commander. A process has begun that will soon let the council elect the city mayor and take direct control of all city departments (where services are currently plagued by corruption and incompetence, under department heads installed by the nepotistic local sheiks).

This election is a happy turn of events. Reflecting the reactionary social structure of the Fallujah area, the council has a much heavier representation of imams and tribal sheiks than other councils I have observed—and here as elsewhere in Iraq, these clan leaders have proved themselves to be parochial, self-interested and generally disappointing. Encouraging this election was something of a risk for the U.S. commanders, for the voting-in of a firebrand could conceivably have been in the cards. Fortunately, even in Fallujah, better educated and more cooperative individuals from the professional and business classes are gradually taking control of the council. The elevation of Dr. Mohammed Hasan al-Balwa to the chair is a further step in this productive direction.

■ ■

The final episode of this marathon meeting features the first-ever public appearance in Fallujah of an official from the Coalition Provisional Authority. Keith Mines sketches the forthcoming transition to Iraqi self-rule, explaining that the CPA plans to dissolve itself at the end of June, at which point the authority's American staff will start to work for the U.S. Embassy.

Mines then outlines the tentative plan for caucuses to select an interim legislature for Anbar Province, the state-like administrative unit of which Fallujah is a part. There will be quotas at the caucuses for the representation of a wide variety of occupations and demographic groups. This brings an intervention from an imam in the audience, who appeals for elimination of the seats for women's affairs, in exchange for additional seats in some other category. He assures the Americans that no woman in all of Fallujah would be willing to travel to Ramadi and appear in public to take part in a provincial caucus of that kind. This elicits an astonished chuckle from Mines, after which the speaker insists, with heads nodding about him, that inquiries have been made, and that certainly no female Fallujans are interested in joining such a council.

This is the kind of issue that must simply be glided over for the moment. Mines wades onward to explain the distinction, not at all clear to his Iraqi questioners, between a legislative and an executive branch, and how the legislature will appoint provincial executives. He fields many questions, and promises to carry local suggestions back to the CPA's Baghdad headquarters.

At one point, the shock wave of a large explosion rocks the building, but Drinkwine continues the meeting with hardly an acknowledgement, as if thunderous explosions were a normal part of city life. (They are in Fallujah.) Quick consultation with a radio operator reveals that the blast was a controlled demolition of confiscated munitions by a U.S. bomb squad. Throughout the afternoon, occasional bursts of automatic gunfire can be heard in other city precincts. By Fallujah's standards, this has so far been a quiet day.

HARD-FOUGHT VICTORY

Around 1600 hours, the councilors quickly depart, and soldiers trickle down from the rooftops and return from foot patrol, piling back into their trucks. Our eighteen-vehicle convoy reorganizes, takes a left out of the youth-center compound and heads down a narrow alley lined with cinderblock walls and heaped garbage. After barely half a block's progress there is suddenly a tremendous boom. I see a spray of earth and smoke jet several stories into the sky just two trucks ahead.

A roadside bomb. Debris rains down on our Humvee, and my right eardrum begins to ache. "Holy s—!" shouts Sergeant Lopez from behind the wheel.

Soldiers leap from the stopped vehicles, fingers on triggers, peering about in every direction for gunmen who might be launching a coordinated ambush. They burst into the house immediately opposite the smoking crater to see if the person who detonated the blast might be there.

It turns out to be a family with small children. Their front gate and windows have been perforated by shrapnel, and water gushes from their shredded water tank. A small child's bicycle lies pathetically on its side amidst shattered glass and chunks of blast debris. Clearly these people didn't set off the bomb; it's a miracle they weren't badly hurt themselves. Once again, the terrorists have shown no concern whatsoever for everyday Iraqis.

Captain Chris Cirino, an explosives expert, scrambles into the four-foot-deep crater and digs up pieces of shrapnel and the remains of a 9-volt battery. A single 155mm artillery shell wired with a blasting cap, he thinks. Amazingly, there are no serious injuries. The IED exploded between two Humvees, and the surrounding earth absorbed much of the blast. The armored windshields of the closest vehicle are shattered, and two soldiers have suffered concussions and hearing loss.

Everyone in the truck is shaken up, but that's all. Providence was smiling this afternoon.

At the Battle Update Brief the next day, the commander of the rifle company that provided the security for the council meeting—a wiry, nervous, intense captain named Caliguire—tells the battalion commander bluntly that he thinks it is tactically dangerous to put soldiers, at an advertised time every week, into a cramped location with only a few exit routes. This is just an invitation for a carefully staged attack.

"Sir, that is the fifth time the platoon hit by that IED has been blasted. They've been very lucky, and they keep getting up and dusting themselves off, but it's only a matter of time until our string runs out. We're taking awful chances to guard these damn council meetings. We're just inviting them to have bombs waiting for us."

Drinkwine hears his officer out and lets some others comment. Then he answers in his placid and careful way: "Look, we've got no choice. That's the only location where these meetings can be held, and we need to have them regularly each week so people come to think of them as part of the fabric of the city's life.

"And I want you to remember something: By getting this governmental body up and running we are beating our opponents. We are showing this whole city that we will not be intimidated. We are showing them that a new era is coming. We are showing them that there is a more productive way. And the enemy's only response is a bomb that mostly hurts an Iraqi family. That's pretty pitiful in the face of what we're accomplishing here. An historic transformation is taking place in this city, and we're in combat to protect it. We've just got to keep fighting through the resistance.

"And listen: I want you officers to tell your troopers that. I want you to tell them why we're doing this. Many of your Joes have no idea what's going on inside that building, and whether it's worth the risks we're taking to be there. Remind them as they're standing exposed on rooftops or walking the streets for four hours why these meetings matter. You tell them we are planting powerful seeds that will change this country forever, so our sons don't have to come back here in the future.

"We've just got to suck it up and do this. These meetings with the council, though often tedious and always dangerous, are vital work. They're one of the ways we are winning this fight."

■ ■

Major Bottiglieri makes a similar point in a different way when I interview him. He draws a bell-shaped curve with a marker on a whiteboard, and says, "This is what Iraqi society looks like—you've got a small population at one end that is openly hostile, and a small population at the opposite end of the curve that is enthusiastically helpful. And then you've got this big bulge in the middle. That middle is where both ends are fighting to draw resources from. The bad guys and the good guys both need to pull from there for intel, physical safety, material and financial resources, and so forth. Right now the middle population is moving more our way than the other way. There are still bad guys out there, but they're losing the battle for the convictions of the middle."

This is happening not only through civic reconstruction work, but also through direct military operations of the sort that Bottiglieri is in charge of planning. "One clear example of military success: The cloverleaf that connects the highway to the main road leading into Fallujah. It used to be perhaps the most dangerous single spot in Iraq, in terms of the number of people killed or wounded there. We had to create a bunch of new ways into the city, by cutting new trails through the desert, just to avoid it.

"But now we've trained the Iraqi police and the ICDC to run off the people who kept planting IEDs there. In the beginning, the new police here used to just sit around the station waiting for something to happen. Now we've got them out walking patrols—a total of 129 different foot patrols across the city.

"And we have taken a lot of bad guys out of circulation. If you look at that original deck of cards of most-wanted Iraqis, there aren't many left out there. The same thing is true here on the local level in Fallujah. There are still plenty of lowlifes who can be hired to carry out attacks. But the evil factions can't regenerate competent leaders fast enough to replace those we're arresting every day.

"There will always be some danger here for us, because it only takes one unbalanced person to stick an IED in the ground. But I can tell you things are getting better. We are winning."

THE PROPAGANDA SHOP

The next day, I observe another successful military operation. Special Forces operators have identified a CD shop in the main market district that is distributing religious extremist and violently anti-Coalition literature and videos. The rifle company from the 10th Mountain Division is assigned to enter the area in force and search the shop.

This is a densely populated and dangerous area. It's immediately adjacent to a commercial block the soldiers call the Weapons Market; earlier this month, a raid there netted two large cargo-trucks-full of RPGs, grenades, assault rifles, and pre-made roadside bombs, available for sale to any customer with cash. As we drive into the neighborhood, we pass what must be a school at recess: a huge mob of kids race across a rubble-strewn lot toward our moving trucks. Most of them are smiling and waving madly. But a few pluck up chunks of concrete and fling them at us. Welcome to Fallujah.

As the morning light begins to intensify, about 150 soldiers unload in an area right next to the Euphrates, several blocks from the Weapons Market area. Leaving behind a rear guard, the rest begin to dash on foot through narrow, garbage-filled alleys, and onto streets crammed with stacks of goods for sale and crowds of staring people. The soldiers have been attacked numerous times in situations like this, and they are tense. "Watch the roofs," shouts one sergeant. "Keep a close eye on our back, gunner," says another. Violence can burst out in a twinkling here, and regularly does. Will this corner bring an ambush? Could that trash heap conceal an IED?

Led by a Special Forces sergeant, we jog to a nondescript storefront on a narrow lane, flanked by shops selling fruit, jewelry, fans, satellite TV dishes and other electronics. The shop is locked and the owner is gone, so one large soldier unslings a battering ram from his shoulder. After two thumps the door is sprung. Arabic-reading soldiers enter the tidy premises and begin to search. Dominating the entranceway is a large poster of pilgrims teeming around the black-shrouded Kaaba in Mecca. Racks of CDs and cassettes cover the other walls. As the searchers rummage through these, they call out titles:

"The Hell of the Russians: Heroes of Chechnya"

"Fallujah Resistance Events of the Quarter"

"Jihad Warriors, by Sabah Hashem"

Hashem is the target of this raid; he owns the shop and has recorded many of the insurrectionist sermons, talks and videos himself. A significant portion of the disks and cassettes have his face plastered on the cover.

"Now we've got to find the recording studio," says one soldier.

"I think this is it," answers another, patting a desktop computer sitting on the counter.

"No, there's a real studio somewhere."

"Our boy has definitely been doing lots of business," comments a trooper combing through a wastebasket. "There are heaps of recent receipts in here with his name on them. I wonder why he threw them away? Maybe heard we were coming and wanted to dump some evidence but we got here too quickly."

"Here's someone who bought fifty-four CDs for 24,000 dinars," reports a soldier looking through a ledger.

"Is there a name?" ask another.

"Yes, it's right here."

"Good, that could lead us somewhere."

One copy of each inflammatory tract, all of the shop's paper records, and the computer are placed in a cardboard box to be carried back to base for further study. Music and other innocuous recordings remain untouched, and great care is taken to avoid messing up the shop or its inventory. When the raiders are done, they even roll down the protective steel storefront covers and flex-lock them in place.

"Prepare for exfiltration," the 10th Mountain captain radios to his soldiers out in the street.

"Sir, the snipers report that a large group of civilians is gathering near our vehicles," relays the radio operator.

"Tell them we're leaving right now."

Just then one of the PsyOps soldiers who has been handing out leaflets to the gathering crowd comes running up to the captain.

"I've found it!"

"What?"

"The recording studio. I was reading the street signs and it's right there, just around the corner. I'll show you."

"Too late now," says the captain. "We're rolling. We'll get it next time."

Just as we're about to depart, the radio hisses with news that an IED has been discovered on the route planned for our exit. This is a favorite tactic of the insurgents: whenever a large force enters the city, quickly booby-trap a likely departure street or two and blow them up on the way out. The commanders select an alternate path.

To circumvent chokepoints at on-ramps, and more generally to avoid following predictable routes where they could be vulnerable to pre-positioned attack, U.S. soldiers have plowed hundreds of new entrances and exits along the divided highways of Iraq. They'll just run a tank or Bradley over a guardrail at some convenient spot—flattening it like an ironed cotton shirt—then take off by a desert shortcut to their next destination. I've even been in Humvees where officers, nervous about getting held up by heavy traffic or just needing access to some particular point, simply ordered their drivers to run up over a guardrail that hadn't yet been squashed down; the goatlike Hummers are quite capable of thumping their way over such obstacles. Consulting their GPS devices, the soldiers will then run cross-country to the next spot where they want to enter a highway, which they'll once again scramble onto without worrying about finding a cloverleaf. This dramatically cuts down ambush opportunities for insurgents.

Halfway home on this trip, the company captain and six gun trucks cut across some open land to visit a gas station on the main highway. Hoarding and black-marketeering led to fuel shortages and gas lines during the summer, sparking many angry complaints from Iraqis; so the soldiers now monitor filling stations closely: Are they getting the deliveries they need? What are they charging per liter? Are they staying open for business throughout the hours advertised? Have they been threatened by black-marketeers recently? The captain will report his findings back to the battalion, which monitors similar reports on the city's other stations.

Another full day for the interim princes of Iraq.

COMING HOME

I have been invited to interview General Swannack at the 82nd's division headquarters at Ramadi. That's about an hour and a half up a highway infested with common bandits and insurgents, so you don't just set off at your convenience. I work out a ride leaving at dawn on a Monday morning on the weekly gravy train that goes up to Ramadi to fetch the battalion's hard spending cash—half a million dollars this week.

But in the middle of the night, a lieutenant comes into the hooch and tells me the trip has been cancelled. That's as much information as you're likely to get in an army at war. The next morning I take a look at my calendar and realize I have a magazine deadline and a college lecture commitment in New York looming, and decide I can't wait for the next shuttle to Ramadi, which could be days. So I walk to the command post and see about mooching a ride to Baghdad International Airport.

I'm in luck: in five minutes a convoy is heading down to the CPA compound in Baghdad. And my new friend Lieutenant Colonel Tony Layton—commander of the 82nd's artillery regiment, who has become a jack-of all trades in this era of guerilla war—is in charge. Yet again I am a beneficiary of soldierly kindness; he tasks a Humvee to peel off from the convoy and deliver me to the airport.

As we roar down the roads (Army drivers roll very fast to make it hard for guerillas to time their IED blasts), we pass a large and very fresh roadside bomb crater, with three American trucks stopped beside it. Someone is examining the hole. An MP waves us past.

Then more luck: prepared to wait for hours or even days on a "space-available" list, I get myself quickly manifested onto a C-130 heading to Kuwait City. With nearly two hours to kill, I pull off an improvised shower, my first in a couple of weeks, and a pure thrill despite no towel, shampoo or any other niceties. After a period of abstinence, simple hot water is the most appreciated element on earth.

Then I find my place on the Air Force cargo plane, settle into the nylon netting that serves as a sling seat, and pull out my laptop to write away the ninety-minute flight out of long-suffering Iraq. It's not until we touch down in Kuwait that I stand and peer into the dark toward the rear of the cargo bay and realize that I've shared this flight not only with thirty-five living U.S. soldiers, but also with a deceased one. There, about twenty feet away, sits a gray metal casket draped with an American flag.

The loadmaster asks us all to remain seated until the fallen warrior is carried off. We remove our headgear. The soldier standing in the receiving truck salutes. The casket slides quietly away behind a curtain draping the vehicle's rear. Then we deplane.

UNDODGEABLE REALITY

At the one-year anniversary of the war that removed Saddam Hussein and set Iraq (and the rest of the Middle East) on a new and uncharted path, 392 American men and women had been killed in action. (Another 187 died in accidents or of natural causes.) Each of these lost sons or husbands or daughters is a source of heartache for their families, and for all Americans. They're also a reminder that, as the saying goes: "Freedom isn't free."

Even back home in our own land, about three hundred defenders of public safety (cops, troopers, sheriffs, firefighters, prison guards) sacrifice their lives every year in the process of protecting the domestic tranquility of our streets, homes and gathering places. That's three thousand traumas per decade, a bill paid far less visibly than war deaths, but just as inexorably. Losses on both battlefronts are part of the blood price of keeping our civilization secure.

Those dead defenders are the reason all decent Americans stand, snatch off their hats, and place their hands on their hearts when old soldiers or officers of the peace walk down our streets at Memorial Day parades or July 4th celebrations. We honor those who bear physical risks for the rest of the country precisely because we know these are not theoretical dangers, but real perils that claim a considerable number of our bravest citizens each season.

The Americans who have given their lives in battle in Iraq aren't random victims. They were doing their duty in one of the great turning points of our generation.

I reached voting age about the time of the Iranian hostage crisis in 1979. What an excruciating episode that was: 52 Americans held against their will, publicly taunted and humiliated day after day, our government paralyzed. And that was just the opening salvo for a generation of Middle Eastern extremism. There was the Beirut barracks bombing that killed 243 Americans. Then the Berlin discotheque blast. The slaughter of 270 innocent people on the terrorist-downed Pan Am Flight 103, plus hundreds more on other sabotaged airplanes. In 1990 came Iraq's rape of Kuwait, and the high costs in blood and treasure of reversing that dangerous thrust. Next was the first attempt to bring down the World Trade Center, in 1993, to which the United States made no effective response at all. Two months later the Iraqi plot to assassinate President Bush was uncovered. Then the Khobar Towers attack in Saudi Arabia murdered American servicemen as they slept. Al-Qaeda helped kill eighteen GIs in Mogadishu, then hundreds of people in two suicide bombings of U.S. embassies in Africa. The near-sinking of the USS *Cole* claimed seventeen sailors and cost tens of millions of dollars. And, finally, the stabbing, singeing, horror of September 11—with all the economic, social and psychic trauma that followed.

Looking back, it's clear that we Americans were slow on the uptake, that we failed over and over again to recognize that this was not a part of the world we could just ignore in the hope it would leave us alone. Only after repeated woundings, followed by one of the ugliest maulings Americans have suffered in their entire three-century history, did we realize that this is a chaotic, hate-filled and violent region which urgently needs to be brought to order by more responsible forces.

Allowing the various zealots who populate the Islamic Middle East to continue their marauding against the rest of the world could, within a period of just a few years, lead to the sort of unimaginable cataclysm that suicidal fanaticism and modern weapons are now able to produce in combination. International inspectors were taken aback to discover in early 2004 how far along the Libyan and Iranian nuclear programs were. At the same time, we learned that the father of Pakistan's "Muslim Bomb" had been selling nuclear secrets even to psychopaths like North Korea's Kim Jong Il over the previous decade. What other nasty surprises await?

A defanging of the Middle East would be a historical event of enormous consequence. And while achieving a positive transformation of the Arab world is undeniably a difficult and risky venture, it is no more unlikely than other dramatic conversions we've witnessed recently: China's shift to capitalism, the elimination of military dictator-ships in Latin America, the end of apartheid, the long-awaited arrival of democracy in Eastern Europe. Squeezing murderous autocracies out of the Islamic crescent and seeding those lands with less threatening forms of govern-ment is not some quixotic crusade or wild goose chase. It is a step that the United States has been pushed to out of self-protection, and if we apply our national attention to the task, it has very reasonable chances of success. It is a fateful summons we cannot turn down.

The unprecedented security, freedom, wealth and opportunity that Americans now enjoy didn't just burst forth out of a cabbage patch. These achievements were created, and then defended many times, by bloody force of arms. If contemporary Americans aren't sturdy enough to bear the sacrifices and tragedies sometimes required in defense of our rare way of life, then we don't deserve our inheritance. That is the undodgeable reality we face today in the Middle East.

THE STRUGGLE OF WILLS

The military men and women with whom I shared my late-January flight back to the United States from Iraq were mostly headed home on emergency leave. A major had lost a grandfather. A sergeant based in Germany was going to collect his family, then fly to Arizona for a relative's funeral. A private quietly explained that his wife, six months pregnant, hadn't felt their first baby move for some time, went to a doctor, and learned they had lost the child. "I'm still in shock. We struggled so hard to conceive."

Not only in war, but also in the safety of our homes, life can often be hard. It is always fleeting. Its meaning comes, ultimately, from the ends toward which it is dedicated.

There are times when the best response, perhaps the only response, to the hard blows of existence is to embrace each lump as a badge honoring the determined striving that produced it. In 1918, Teddy Roosevelt's son Quentin (who had left Harvard during his sophomore year to serve in World War I) was shot out of the sky in one of aerial warfare's early dogfights. German propagandists took photos of his maimed body amidst his plane's wreckage and, hoping to dampen American morale, sent one to Mrs. Roosevelt. Rather than let herself be cowed, however, she insisted that the picture be framed and displayed over a mantelpiece, a symbol of her family's sturdiness and their pride in sacrifice for a high cause.

As I traveled across Iraq with our soldiers, I thought of this incident. What Edith Roosevelt did was both a very hard and a very soft thing. She pushed aside her own grief and expressed admiration and undying love for her son by celebrating his bravery—and by refusing to abandon his fight.

One paradoxical aspect of greatness is that it is not necessarily built on dominating power. It is often the "softer" varieties of strength that are most important in achieving high ends. Biblical virtues like humility, altruism, and endurance in the face of anguish are often essential when leading a society into new territory.

There is a story of an angry conqueror addressing an unbending priest in his overrun village. "Don't you know I'm the one who can have you torn apart without batting an eye?" he threatened.

To which the priest replied, as a devout Christian: "Don't you know that I'm the one who can *be* torn apart without batting an eye?"

The Irish rebel leader Terence MacSwiney once wrote that "It is not those who can inflict the most but those who can suffer the most who will conquer." At the root of many successful political struggles, myriad break-throughs in science, much great literature and art, and most successful military actions you will find a very simple, humble and stubborn quality: endurance.

Being a successful leader usually involves less flash, triumph, and acclaim than is often imagined. What separates successful, influential people and nations from others, quite frequently, is simply their ability never to be crushed—to absorb disappointment, hurt and failure, and turn these into something productive. That may be the highest test of leadership.

For even a fortunate existence will be studded with trials. The strong cope with these setbacks with patience, with moral sturdiness, and with a willingness to sacrifice immediate happiness to defend long-term principles. These are the qualities that have animated great leaders, triumphant warriors and remarkable nations throughout history.

Do the United States and its small circle of fighting allies still possess this enduring strength deep in our bones? British prime minister Tony Blair recently noted that the terrorists doubt we have the fortitude for a nasty fight. "One thing is for sure: the extremists have faith in our weakness just as they have faith in their own religious fanaticism. And the weaker we are, the more they will come after us."

As they aggressively attack ancient evil and gently nurture frail shoots of a new good, our military bear many risks in Iraq. They face enemies who aim to kill them and to panic the American public standing behind them. Our battle against Middle Eastern extremism can thus be thought of as a struggle of wills.

But demoralization can work both ways—and today it is Iraq's insurgents who are facing physical and psychological defeat. In January, U.S. forces seized a letter written by al-Qaeda's mastermind in Iraq, Abu Musab al-Zarqawi, as it was being carried by a courier to top al-Qaeda leaders in Afghanistan. The seventeen-page document despairs that despite their deadly car bombs and the sporadic killing of U.S. troops, the guerillas have managed neither to push the Americans from Iraq, nor to spark mass discord among Iraqis. The letter reports that the insurgents are having trouble convincing Iraqis to join their resistance, and mourns that American forces show "no intention of leaving, no matter how many wounded." He continues:

> There is no doubt that our field of movement is shrinking.... With the spread of the army and police, our future is becoming frightening.... Our enemy is growing stronger day after day, and its intelligence information increases. By God, this is suffocation!

Al-Qaeda itself is now in shambles. Two-thirds of its leaders have been killed or captured, the survivors are on the run, finances have collapsed, communication has been strangled, recruiting is difficult. Iraq's Baath Party has likewise been eviscerated. Our incursions into Afghanistan and Iraq have not only eliminated two terror-sponsoring regimes but have also directly liberated fifty million people from two of the most oppressive regimes in history.

And in so doing, we have turned other bullies in the region in skittish and newly cooperative directions. Libyan ruler Muammar Qaddafi telephoned Italian prime minis-

ter Silvio Berlusconi last year and told him, "I will do whatever the Americans want, because I saw what happened
in Iraq and I was afraid." There is evidence that Syria has
moderated its behavior. With the installation of a prime
minister, the Palestinians have begun to fumble for some
alternative to Yasser Arafat. Iran's mullahs are clearly on
edge as democratic reformers, emboldened by the freeing
of Iraq, step up their demands; and the Europeans, pushed
by American decisiveness, have rushed to convince Iran
to open its secret nuclear program to international inspec-
tions. The nuclear proliferation network run by the Pak-
istani scientist A. Q. Khan has been broken up. The Saudis
have agreed to hold new municipal elections, Jordan is
accelerating market-based reforms, and Qatar is reform-
ing its education system.

These are fruits of American action.

While the United States will need to battle against terror for years to come, it is finally on offense, not defense.
Since we brought the battle to the plotters in their own
strongholds, things have remained thankfully quiet at
home. And across the Middle East, the most desperate
effort of a range of terrorist elements is now to avoid U.S.
forces.

"We are at a breaking point today," Colonel Fuller tells
me, leaning forward for emphasis in his Baghdad headquarters. "This insurgency is running out of steam. We
see many signs that Iraqis want the violence to be over.
They want to get on with their lives. They can see we are
not quitting, and they are increasingly willing to cooperate, come forward to help us, and stand up to the worst
elements in their society."

This progress has been won by thousands of U.S. soldiers doing their duty in Iraq. If Americans back at home will exhibit the tough love of the steely Mrs. Roosevelt—celebrating the accomplishments of our sons and daughters by cherishing their sacrifices on our mantels, and multiplying and extending their courage by refusing to abandon the struggle they are waging—then this is a fight America will certainly win.

AUTHOR'S NOTE

THE MEDIA WAR

The Iraq war, like other guerilla wars, is only partly a military fray. The other half of the battle is psychological and cultural—and imagery is a central part of this. In the new style of fighting that America is having to pursue in the war on terror (a struggle that will occupy us for at least the next decade), the contest over images will be crucial.

There are negative impressions of the United States that need to be addressed. That's why our government has international broadcasting and "public diplomacy" programs that aim to bring a fairer picture of our society to Middle Easterners who have been marinated, indeed pickled, in folk myths hostile to the U.S. (Americans hate Islam; they don't let Arabs vote; their women are all trollops; most Americans are atheists; they want Israel to control Mecca; U.S. soldiers abuse Muslim women; they disrespect Muslim culture; they are going to seize the Middle East's oil fields; etc.) It's important that America respond to these myths (accepted even by many educated persons in the Middle East) with more accurate counter-images of American ideals, our institutions and our citizenry.

There is one point of view—I'm told it is represented very strongly on the U.S. government's Broadcasting Board of Governors, which supervises our overseas broadcasting efforts—that suggests it was MTV that toppled the Berlin Wall, and that American pop culture's seductive appeal will next tear down the Lambskin Curtain ringing the Islamic world. By this logic, Janet Jackson is our secret weapon.

This is a very dubious claim, and probably gets things exactly backwards. Pushing pop culture as America's quintessence only validates the hysterical claims of Islamists: "If you buy into American-style political and economic freedom, quicker than you can say 'decadence' your daughters will be baring their breasts on television, and your sons will be marrying other sons at city hall."

A more serious and fruitful view of the image war is that the United States needs to treat Middle Eastern paranoia with the medicine of straightforward documentary truth. That was the motivation behind the embedding program that allowed more than six hundred reporters to accompany American troops throughout the spring 2003 war. These, by the way, included thirteen reporters from al-Jazeera, numerous French and other European TV crews, and hundreds of other foreign journalists.

When I first heard about the unprecedented level of access being offered to embedded reporters, I assumed that some bold risk-taker like Don Rumsfeld must have pushed the idea. I was wrong. The impetus, I discovered, actually came from U.S. commanders themselves, particularly officers who had been burned by disinformation in Afghanistan. Right after American forces left a village, Taliban elements would often swoop in just in time to tell freshly arriving reporters that the soldiers had committed atrocities, killed innocents or raped women. The officers realized that if they had neutral third-party witnesses with them, such spurious claims and rumors would be nipped in the bud.

Having nothing to hide, U.S. commanders decided that during their fight in Iraq, they would take their chances with a policy of extreme openness. Better to risk occasional security breaches than to let civilian populations whose cooperation was needed think the worst of us. And so embedded journalists were allowed, for the first time, to give global audiences direct and unfiltered access to the actual events of the hot war in Iraq.

There were a few highly tendentious critics, nearly all of them hotel or studio reporters who never got anywhere near the action in Iraq, who worried that the embedding process gave the Pentagon a chance to brainwash and manipulate journalists. All six hundred of us! "Is there a 'Stockholm syndrome' in which journalists start to identify with the soldiers and lose their professional detachment?" twittered academics Stephen Hess and Marvin Kalb.

Nearly all fair-minded observers, however—including most reporters—eventually concluded that the embedded reporting was the least problematic journalism of the war. Far worse was the Monday morning quarterbacking of the studio- and office-bound pundits back in the States. One of my favorite bits of armchair criticism was NPR correspondent Tom Gjelten's priceless statement on March

21—exactly one day after troops crossed the Kuwait border into Iraq—that "if the war is still going on a week
from now, that will be a bad sign." Here's a guy who I'm
willing to bet has never won a fistfight, let alone a battle,
telling Americans that if it takes more than a week to sub-
due a nation bigger than the entire northeastern United
States, that constitutes failure.

By the end of March, many of Gjelten's fellow lem-
mings were following the same gloomy line. On April 1,
Robert Wright of the online magazine *Slate* diagnosed "the
Pentagon's failure to send enough troops to take Baghdad"
with great authority. "As the war drags on," he droned, "as
more civilians die and more Iraqis see their resistance hailed
across the Arab world as a watershed in the struggle against
Western imperialism, the traditionally despised Saddam
could gain appreciable support among his people." That
same week in April, Seymour Hersh of the *New Yorker* (who
has filed enough false reports and way-off predictions over
the years to justify a new Guinness Book entry for unreli-
ability) charged that "Rumsfeld simply failed to anticipate
the consequences of protracted warfare. He put Army and
Marine units in the field with few reserves and an insuffi-
cient number of tanks." Actually, U.S. forces entered Baghdad on April 5—before the April 7 magazine issue
containing Hersh's analysis was even on the newsstands.

Around the same time, the BBC aired claims that the
U.S. "could take, bluntly, a couple to three thousand casu-
alties" during the invasion. In the event, the number of
U.S. soldiers killed was considerably less than two hundred.

Syndicated columnist Michelle Malkin had an interesting idea in mid-April. She decided to compare the

defeatist reports being published in much of the liberal press with images being sent back from the front by photographers. Quoting from the captions on photos from all parts of Iraq, she found that Iraqis were receiving Americans much more warmly than the simultaneous news copy implied. The pictures showed that things weren't nearly so bad as reporters claimed.

Compared with media predictions, the actual course of the hot war was a story of the dog that didn't bark. Many of the journalists I crossed paths with in Kuwait prior to the outbreak of hostilities were confidently predicting that the *fedayeen* would create killer floods by breaking the dams west of Baghdad, that the oil fields would be destroyed, that Iraq's multifarious ethnic and religious groups would be at each other's throats, that Turkey might occupy the north, that Israel could well strike from the south, that the Arab "street" would roar in resistance. As the Americans poured north, none of these things happened.

Not only was the hot war itself vastly less bloody and difficult than claimed, but the immediate aftermath was also quieter. We were told to expect a refugee flood, a food crisis, burning oil wells, and public health and environmental catastrophes. The months since May 1, 2003, have hardly been a cakewalk, but thankfully these traumatic prophecies turned out to be baseless.

"Contrary to the predictions," points out media critic Brent Bozell, "there were no homeland terrorist attacks, no chemical gassings of the troops, no mass mobilization of Arab killers, no 100-percent-of-the-vote fierce support for Saddam Hussein, no quagmire of unending length, no public-opinion debacle for President Bush, no hopelessly fractured alliances. But being a journalist," he continues, "means never having to say you're sorry."

For some journalists, it also means never having to admit you're a nincompoop. Take a whiff of the megalomaniacal egotism in this statement at the peak of the hot war in March 2003 by TV correspondent Peter Arnett:

> The first plan has failed ... clearly the American war planners misjudged the determination of Iraqi forces. And I personally do not understand how that happened, because I've been there many times and in my commentaries on television I would tell the Americans about the determination of the Iraqi forces.... But me, and others who felt the same way, were not listened to by the Bush administration.

That's five instances of "I," "me" or "my" in three sentences. It's a wonder that the boys finally managed to complete the liberation without Peter about one week later—after Arnett himself was fired for an even more tasteless interview aired on Iraqi TV, bordering on pro-Saddam propaganda.

Of course, no respectable media outlet should have sent Peter Arnett to the Middle East in the first place—for he has a long history of making false claims and unsupported inflammatory statements. This is the same journalist who convinced America, completely erroneously, that a Viet Cong squad occupied the U.S. Embassy during the Tet Offensive, who in 1991 peddled Iraqi misinformation about a "baby milk factory" being bombed by Americans, the man who aired a famously untrue report on CNN claiming that the U.S. military had used nerve gas on defectors in Vietnam, and who once said he would let GIs die rather than reveal enemy plans he had discovered as a journalist. It was a bad enough idea for the TV establishment to send fluffernutters like Geraldo Rivera to Iraq; using the thoroughly discredited Peter Arnett was out-and-out malpractice.

WHY IRAQ?

The most insistent bit of media second-guessing over the last year has centered on the failure of the Coalition to find weapons of mass destruction in Iraq. It appears that Western intelligence on this subject was dated and inaccurate. Amidst the drumbeat of charges that the WMD threat was cooked up in the White House, it needs to be pointed out that the Democrats in Congress were looking at the same intelligence provided to George Bush, and that the French, German and other international intelligence services made the same guesses we did, coming to the conclusion that Saddam was dangerous and probably had biological and chemical weapons.

Here's what John Kerry said in a major Georgetown University speech a month before the Iraq invasion:

> Without question, we need to disarm Saddam Hussein.... He is miscalculating America's response to his continued deceit and his consistent grasp for weapons of mass destruction.... The threat of Saddam Hussein with weapons of mass destruction is real.

And here's what the *New York Times* Monday morning quarterbacks now criticizing the decision to go into Iraq were saying back on Sunday morning (February 2003):

> There is ample evidence that Iraq has produced highly toxic VX nerve gas and anthrax and has the capacity to produce a lot more.... Iraq is not disarming.... [T]he Security Council is united in its determination to disarm him and is now ready to call in the cavalry to get the job done. America and Britain are prepared to take that step. The time has come for the others to quit pretending that inspections alone are the solution.... The Security Council doesn't need to sit through more months of inconclusive reports. It needs full and immediate Iraqi disarmament. It needs to say so, backed by the threat of military force.

My own view on the question of Iraq's weapons of mass destruction is simple. Without question, we need to improve the quality of U.S. intelligence on the Islamic world, and if that requires shaking up some agencies, or spending more money, or removing some of the foolish strictures we imposed on ourselves during the 1970s left-wing crusades against the CIA, then this is what we must do. But when it came time, after toppling the Taliban, to decide where the United States should move next in its post-9/11 campaign to clean up Middle Eastern extremism, knowing whether Saddam Hussein possessed WMDs in March 2003 was not terribly important.

After all, we know he possessed such weapons in the past—and indeed demonstrated on more than forty different occasions that he was quite willing to *use* them, killing thousands of his own people as well as Iranians. Clearly this was a man entirely capable of making and using them again in the future. So whether his regime was actively producing chemical, biological or nuclear weapons last year, or whether they had supplies buried somewhere, or whether they slipped their weapons across the Syrian border—these are issues of timing, not the heart of the matter. The heart of the matter is that Saddam was utterly uncontrite about his past transgressions, and could be expected to produce horrible weapons in the future. Given his psychopathic nature and the post-9/11 perils, why hazard that?

"There are a thousand hacking at the branches of evil to one who is striking at the root," Thoreau once complained. Regimes like Saddam Hussein's, which have produced a whole generation of homicidally frustrated young men, are the very root of today's evil in the Muslim world. And didn't September 11 convince us that dangers from that quarter cannot be ignored? Charles Krauthammer sketched this broader aspect of the Iraq war in his 2004 Irving Kristol Lecture:

> Yes, the undertaking is enormous, ambitious, and may fail. But we can't afford not to try. There is not a single, remotely plausible alternative strategy for attacking the monster behind 9/11—which is not Osama bin Laden, but the cauldron of political oppression, religious intolerance, and social ruin in the Arab-Islamic world. Oppression deflected by regimes with no legitimacy into virulent, murderous anti-Americanism. The cops-and-robbers law-enforcement model of fighting terrorism that we tried for 20 years gave us 9/11. This is war, and in war you win by taking territory—and leaving something behind.

Of course, the Taliban and the Baathists weren't the only sources of evil in the Middle East. I will grant that there was a degree of arbitrariness in the decision to war against Saddam Hussein—there are other ruling gangs in the region that are almost as illegitimate and dangerous. One could just about flip open a Middle Eastern atlas at random, jab a pin into any page, and say, "let's start the clean-up here." But there are two reasons that Iraq was an especially good place to start the effort to reverse the region's extremism: 1) Saddam was the very baddest of the bad, a kind of human WMD who had killed hundreds of thousands and encouraged others with similar propensities, as well as a kleptomaniac on a scale of billions of dollars; and 2) Iraq has the human and natural resources to become a very different, much better place within a reasonable amount of time, setting an example that others could follow.

Sorting out a new future for Iraq is much harder than pillorying the U.S. and British leaders for being wrong about Saddam's WMDs—but also more important. Playing "gotcha" with last year's intelligence estimates may produce the kind of human dramas that reporters relish, but it doesn't bring any progress on America's most important foreign mission in a generation.

NEGATIVITY WITHOUT BALANCE

I'm hardly the only one to be concerned about the unbalanced negativity in media coverage of the war in Iraq. About six months into the guerilla phase of the struggle,

Jim Keelor, president of Liberty Broadcasting, which owns eight NBC television stations, wrote to NBC News executives complaining that "the networks are pretty much ignoring" any positive news from the land of the Tigris and Euphrates. A proper "definition of news would incorporate some of these stories," he urged. The failure of the major networks to provide such balance in their coverage, he warned, was the cause of the meteoric surge of viewers to his competitor FOX News over the previous year.

Bob Arnot, an NBC correspondent himself, entered a similar objection in December 2003, complaining that NBC's coverage had been much more negative than events on the ground justified. Many stories of successful operations that he reported in Iraq were rejected, he told NBC News president Neal Shapiro in an e-mail later revealed in the *New York Observer*. Arnot objected that NBC's blinders were "allowing the terrorists to fight their war on the American television screen, where their stories of death and destruction dominate."

In early 2004, a producer for MSNBC wrote an exposé after his return from Iraq stating that American TV reporters do hardly any reporting from the field. They rarely leave their heavily guarded hotels in central Baghdad, said Noah Oppenheim; most of their stories are just conventional wisdom and casualty tales taken from wire reports, regurgitated in front of convenient film backdrops. For his frankness in the pages of the *Weekly Standard*, Oppenheim was forced from his job by Tom Brokaw and *NBC Nightly News* producer Steve Capus.

Negative sensationalism is a perennial weakness of journalism. I lived in Ireland for a couple of years amidst the worst troubles with the IRA. Many times, Irish people came up to me and asked why the international news media reported on Ireland as if the whole country were in flames, when in reality the violence was quite localized.

But when it comes to Iraq, there is not only a bad-news bias in place, but a journalistic establishment that resists correction. Often, the distortion is unintentional, or at least unconscious. Consider the front-page *New York Times* story of October 25, 2003, which announced that the U.S. had won commitments of money from many nations "for reconstruction of water, power, health care, and other systems devastated by the American invasion six months ago." In truth, these systems were almost entirely untouched by the war (thanks to careful efforts by U.S. military commanders). Their decrepitude today is a result of mismanagement and embezzling by Saddam's managers, chronic lack of maintenance, and years of sanctions—as the *Times* itself was forced to admit two days later in a small correction box stating that their article "referred incorrectly to the factors that depleted Iraq's" basic infrastructure.

Likewise, the *New York Times* has for months been reprinting a claim that Baghdad's murder rate stands at a sky-high average of around 150 killings per 100,000 residents per year. When economist and crime statistician John Lott inquired how this had been calculated, he discovered it was an exceedingly crude estimate derived, without any sensible adjustments, from the number of bodies passing through the Baghdad morgue—which includes deaths like automobile fatalities, suicides, accidents, and insurgent fighters killed by U.S. soldiers.

Figuring the murder rate in Washington, D.C., by the *Times*'s method, Lott calculated, would yield a figure of up to twenty times the true homicide level.

Lott pointed all this out to the *Times* in two separate letters, sent in November 2003 and February 2004. He also informed the editors that better data, collected by lawyers from the U.S. Army 1st Armored Division in Baghdad using American crime definitions, was available, and that this showed Baghdad's 2003 murder rate to be only 16 per 100,000 (and tumbling rapidly through the course of the year). His letters and phone calls were ignored.

The misleading defeatism of today's Iraq reporting concerns observers of many stripes. Don Walter, the retired federal judge who traveled the Fertile Crescent to assess the Iraqi legal system, notes that initially, he "vehemently opposed the war," and that only after visiting scores of sites and talking to hundreds of Iraqis did he conclude that America is a strongly positive force in the country. After returning from his work in Iraq, he complained that "we are not getting the whole truth from the news media. The news you watch, listen to, and read is highly selective. . . . I fear we will quit as the horrors of war come into our living rooms. . . . The steady drip, drip, drip of bad news may destroy our will to fulfill the obligations we have assumed."

A similar observation was made late in 2003 by another independent official recently returned from Iraq—Congressman Jim Marshall, a Democrat who serves on the House Armed Services Committee and a Vietnam combat veteran. "I'm afraid the news media are hurting our chances. They are dwelling upon the mistakes, the ambushes, the soldiers killed, the wounded," he wrote in the *Atlanta Journal-Constitution*. Fresh from an inspection tour across Iraq, he warned that reporters are "not balancing this bad news with 'the rest of the story,' the progress made daily, the good news. The falsely bleak picture weakens our national resolve, discourages Iraqi cooperation, and emboldens our enemy."

Tony Blair went even further in April 2004. He warned that there are important Western journalists, politicians and other elites who wish that President Bush or "the power of America" would be defeated in Iraq. "The truth is," wrote Blair in Britain's *Observer,* "faced with this struggle on which our own fate hangs, a significant part of Western opinion is sitting back—if not half-hoping we fail—certainly replete with *schadenfreude* at the difficulty we find."

DISTORTION DANGERS

Yet another demurrer is former *Wall Street Journal* arts writer Steven Vincent. After spending weeks among "Baghdad's bohemians—young, smart painters, poets, and sculptors comfortable with English and familiar with foreign reporters," he summarized the experiences of these Iraqis with international reporters.

> These young Iraqi artists—moderate, pro-Western, eager to join the international community—are the kind of people who are crucial to Iraq's move toward democracy. So why don't the world media focus more on such figures instead of just the disgruntled ex-Baathists and religious firebrands? . . . As painter Esam Pasha told me,

226

"Many journalists act as if they know all the answers. They just need us to make negative comments about the U.S." Sometimes this bias produces manipulation of facts. One painter recounted how a German TV journalist reported that an ash-strewn field was once "farmland destroyed by Coalition bombing"—even though the painter protested that the field was the trash heap for a nearby village. Sculptor Haider Wady recalled how a Spanish photographer he was accompanying as a translator posed an Iraqi woman amidst a dilapidated building and asked her to raise her hands in sorrowful supplication. "The photographer first asked the woman to remove her expensive wristwatch," Wady said. "When I pointed out that she had a car and was in fact pretty wealthy, the photographer ignored me. She just wanted to make the U.S. look bad."

As his own example of "how appallingly one-sided some of the Western reporting has become," Tony Blair cites press coverage of the April 2004 agitations by Iraqi extremist cleric Moktada Sadr. He notes that "the Iraqi judge who issued a warrant for Sadr's arrest, in connection with the murder of a more moderate cleric last year," is a courageous individual who "has braved assassination attempts in order to follow proper judicial process." Yet many reporters "dismissed him as an American stooge."

I can tell you from a full year's interaction and correspondence with soldiers who have served in Iraq that this sort of thing drives them up the wall. I've received many letters similar to this one from Lieutenant Nathan Woodside of the First Marine Division (a unit involved in both the 2003 hot war and the 2004 counterinsurgency in Iraq).

I get very frustrated with the media.... I don't think I'll ever again be the voracious news consumer I was before.... These journalists come in for a day or two, never get out of their SUVs to walk around or go into people's homes, or play with kids at schools. They hear that a soldier was killed by a sniper. Power went out. People took to the streets to protest.... Then all of a sudden this place is "unstable" and "a quagmire." How many American cities are "unstable" and stuck in a "quagmire"? By the media's definition, I'd say quite a few. What would today's American journalists have said about the months after the American Revolution, Reconstruction in the South, even post-Nazi Germany? How have these educated journalists become so short-sighted and pessimistic?

You can't change a country in a few months.... The months after combat have had their ups and downs and struggles. We expected that.... The bottom line is this: Things are not as bad as they appear on the news. I can't believe how bad the press is.

Max Boot of the Council on Foreign Relations, author of a perceptive book on guerilla conflicts and one of the more perspicacious observers of events in Iraq over the last year, had this to say in the *Los Angeles Times* immediately after returning from travels in Iraq:

I couldn't help but see parallels with Vietnam. But not in the way you'd think. Usually Vietnam is invoked to warn of a quagmire, of an impending U.S. defeat against a guerilla foe. El Salvador, Haiti, Bosnia, Kosovo, and Afghanistan were all going to be the "next" Vietnam before winding up as U.S. victories. Now it's Iraq's turn to be seen, unfairly, as the looming quagmire. But the real parallel with Vietnam is the disparity between battlefield realities and home-front perceptions.

The deepest risk of inadequate and skewed reporting from Iraq is what might be called the "Tet Offensive syndrome." This 1968 sneak attack by the Viet Cong was presented in the major American media as a big setback for the U.S. military. From that point onward, the unalterable conventional wisdom was that Vietnam was inevitably lost to communist guerillas. A minority of voices at the time insisted that the Tet Offensive was actually a crushing defeat for the Viet Cong, and historians with subsequent access to actual war records have confirmed that the Viet Cong were nearly wiped out by the U.S. counteroffensive. But a few televised images of attacks on the U.S. Embassy, underscored by Walter Cronkite's emphatic insistence that America was taking a beating, were what sunk into the public consciousness. America's will to fight collapsed, and within a few years the predictions of defeat became a self-fulfilling prophecy.

LIFE ON URANUS

Why are so many reporters more pessimistic about Iraq than most of the soldiers, reconstruction experts, foreign service officials, congressmen of both parties, embedded-journalist dissenters like myself, and others who have had extensive experience in the country? Part of it is the media's structural bias in favor of bad news. Part of it is just the deep cynicism that many journalists bring to their job.

Part of it is laziness. Explosions and fires are simple stories; it takes time, and creativity, to tell the deeper, protracted story of Iraqi reconstruction. Getting out into the countryside and amongst the soldiers doing the fighting is dangerous and dirty work; it's much easier to hang around the one or two hotels in Baghdad where nearly all the elite media cluster, repeating the same hoary storylines to each other.

And part of the media's negativity on Iraq is also political coloration. Two decades' worth of evidence have now piled up showing that most elite journalists vote the same way—on the liberal side of the spectrum. For instance, a 1996 survey of 139 elite Washington, D.C., journalists conducted by the widely respected Roper Center found that Democrats outnumbered Republicans by more that 12 to 1, and that they voted for Clinton over Bush the elder by 89 percent to 7 percent (a ratio of nearly 13 to 1). When *U.S. News and World Report*'s Kenneth Walsh personally surveyed the White House press corps for a 1996 book, he found they voted by 8:2 for Carter over Reagan in 1980; by 10:0 for Mondale over Reagan in 1984; by 12:1 for Dukakis over Bush in 1988; by 9:2 for Clinton over Bush in 1992.

The Roper Center, working under commission from an advocacy organization for journalists (the Freedom Forum), found that 61 percent of national reporters identify themselves as "liberal," while just 9 percent call themselves "conservative." This lack of ideological diversity produces herd behavior. And it means that errors of perspective tend to pile up mostly on one end of the political scale.

Even apart from politics, reporters are extreme pack animals, and much more inbred than many viewers and readers realize. They tend to have similar backgrounds and worldviews, and most rely on the same professional techniques. Most live in constant panic that a colleague will pick up some rumor before they do, so they tend to cling together in tight bunches, spending far too much time gossiping with each other and the hired nationals who form the driver/translator/fixer bubble around them (choosing much of what they do and see), and not nearly enough time out in the field with the hoi polloi. In the case of TV journalists there is the additional fact that many of them are, well, not the sharpest knives in the drawer—a factor exacerbated by the celebrity narcissism that TV encourages.

There is also the basic cultural divide that separates most reporters from fighting men and their work. My friend and fellow reporter Kate O'Beirne put this in a nutshell recently: "You've got to remember, most of these journalists spent their high school years being stuffed into lockers by the kind of males who are now running our military operations in Iraq." The soldier's life is unfathomable, and often threatening, to a typical journalist. But of course the journalists control the pens, cameras and microphones that form our nation's image of what's happening in the Middle East, so they get the last word.

I consider it unhealthy that such a divide has grown up between the population that fights our wars and the population that writes about them. In the past this gap wasn't so wide. As recently as the late 1950s there were more than a thousand students at Stanford (to take just one example) who were enrolled in the ROTC program. That resulted in lots of overlap between the people who ended up running our military and the people who staffed our newsrooms, law offices, legislative chambers and so forth. But during the Vietnam period, the ROTC building at Stanford was burned by protesters, and the program was booted off campus and never allowed to return. Today there are only twenty-nine Stanford students in ROTC, and all of them pull that off with considerable difficulty by taking their training off campus.

At most of the other elite universities where the majority of our journalists are now produced, the same phenomenon holds true. While nearly seven hundred Harvard students were killed in World War II, only twenty died fighting in Vietnam; even fewer serve now. At most Ivy League campuses today you can count on one hand the number of graduating seniors who enter the military.

Faculty members with military experience are even rarer. For example, George Zilbergeld, a professor at Montclair State University (the second largest college in New Jersey, after Rutgers, with more than 13,000 students) realized recently that he is one of only six faculty members at his institution who are veterans. And most of those six, he told reporter Brendan Conway, found it necessary to conceal their military experience from their fellow baby-boomer academics in order to get hired and tenured.

An intellectual class lacking experience of military life will make errors of both omission and commission when analyzing great events like the Iraq war. Professor Rodney

Stark notes that for generations, academic historians missed many critical lessons in military history simply because they didn't understand the importance of the invention of the stirrup to cavalry warfare. It wasn't until 1931, when an amateur historian and highly experienced French cavalry officer named Lefebvre de Noettes began to write about saddles, harnesses, horseshoes and other accouterments, that scholars began to see why crucial clashes in ancient and medieval times had gone as they did.

One way that military illiteracy in the media leads to misportrayal is through unrealistic expectations. My friend Michael Barone of *U.S. News* has castigated reporters for applying what he calls the "zero defect standard" to the prosecution of the battles. Why weren't we "ready" for the looting? Why didn't we just stop it? Why the shortages of electric power and gasoline? Why couldn't we predict the unfolding of the insurgency? Why are so many weapons still floating around the country? Why didn't somebody "do something" about the IED threat?

Right from the earliest days of the Iraq battles, one of the main media criticisms has been that the war "plans" were inadequate. Such statements make soldiers laugh. They know that warfighting is, by definition, a messy, unpredictable, free-form, constantly changing process. You have to adapt on the fly, over and over again. Soldiers realize it can take years to win a war. They know that pacifying and rebuilding Japan took most of a decade. They remember that Germany didn't hold an election until four years after World War II had ended. U.S. soldiers and administrators serving in Iraq understand that they are turning a tide of history and culture in the Middle East, and they are not surprised that one year after crossing the Kuwaiti border they are still slugging it out in some places. They are pleased to have accomplished so much, so fast.

Game plans, boundaries, rules and referees are for the suburban soccer matches of reporters' kids. Wars are more rough-and-ready than that. Assessing the liberation of a large country as if it were a scripted play is unfair, and will only lead to misimpressions and overlooked accomplishments. Soldiers look at the hard-won achievements in Iraq and see a half-full glass, while reporters, clueless as to the nature and difficulty of low-intensity urban conflict, see half-empty. Military leaders are from Mars, most journalists are from Uranus.

THEY REPORT, THEY DECIDE?

To be sure, a critical or skeptical temperament is central to the work of a journalist. Reporting for evening news broadcasts and the front pages of newspapers, however, should never veer into criticism per se. The temptation to confuse advocacy with reporting has snared far too many contemporary journalists. They experience the heady thrill of playing critic, expert, pundit, then drift beyond the boundaries of their fact-gathering profession, stepping into the realm of policymaking.

Criticism is easy, but it is responsible proponents sticking out their necks who ultimately solve problems. "Any jackass can kick down a barn," Lyndon Johnson once observed. "It takes a hard-working carpenter to erect one." Politicians, generals, civilian contractors—these laborers in Iraq are ultimately accountable for their decisions, counsel, actions and achievements. But who holds the media accountable for their claims?

Because our media are self-appointed and unrecallable, it is to a considerable degree only other reporters who can hold reporters to account. That's why it is so important that our newsrooms be balanced, with a mix of intellectual perspectives. Unfortunately, elite reporters today are far too homogeneous and nationally unrepresentative in their backgrounds and ideologies. When the vast number of press corps critics start from the same political perspective (as they now do in 12 out of 13 cases), when most are culturally separated from the objects of their scrutiny (as most reporters are from soldiers), when they lack practical expertise (as too many media pontificators do), then the value of their critiques is limited.

When I make arguments like these, the reaction of my fellow reporters generally falls somewhere between hand-waving dismissal and rage. My observations in my book *Boots on the Ground* about failed and tendentious reporting I observed during the hot war in Iraq produced some angry attacks and got me blacklisted at several publications. Given that journalists make a living critiquing and not infrequently ridiculing other institutions, professions and people, I suggest they have no right to be thin-skinned about being criticized themselves. But they are.

In particular, members of the media establishment refuse to take seriously any arguments identifying media bias. It's a subject they hate. They will simply roll their eyes, ignore you in blacked-out silence if they can get away with it, or pronounce you a member of "the right-wing conspiracy" if you manage to garner any attention for your assessment. Top reporters and editors are an extremely clubby group, and they punish anyone who doesn't close ranks with the club whenever its fairness and competence come into question.

There is one gaping flaw in their strategy: The public is on the side of the critics. I won't repeat the figures and polling data that I assembled in *Boots on the Ground* documenting the public's unhappiness with contemporary journalism. But I will note that there's a reason why journalists come out at the very bottom in public rankings of confidence in various professions. There is a reason that 72 percent of Americans now say "the news media have too much power and influence." There is a reason large majorities of the public think that news organizations are "unhelpful" in solving national problems, more "inaccurate" than "accurate," and "unwilling to admit mistakes." The American public graded our major networks, newspapers and magazines pretty harshly for the way they covered the spring 2003 war in Iraq, and many have migrated in disgust to alternate sources of information for coverage of the guerilla war.

This public disaffection will continue and expand until our news aristocrats address the structural distortions that plague their coverage of subjects like the Iraq war. An important task in the meantime is to make sure that the public's reaction to media cynicism doesn't drag down other institutions and critical national projects. Like the effort to shape a safer Middle East—a high and worthy cause that too many good Americans have bled for to let it be done in by snipers plinking from keyboards.

There are some reporters who understand this. One of the best—unfortunately no longer exerting his salutary influence on our profession since perishing in April 2003 while embedded with U.S. soldiers in Iraq—was Michael Kelly. In a 1997 column for the *Washington Post* he warned that "my generation of reporters" (he was a baby boomer) "is, in matters military ... forever suffering a collective case of the vapors. At the least exposure to the most unremarkable facts of military life ... we are forever shocked." Sounding very much like Edith Roosevelt, he went on to point out that journalists who exhibit knee-jerk hostility to war, even righteous war, overlook something critical: "Accepting death is indispensable to defeating death." There are fewer and fewer people among American elites, he worried, who perceive what even twelve-year-olds in less coddled places understand: "That there are things worth dying for."

It is in Kelly's spirit that I offer this critique of the last year's Iraq war journalism. Indeed, it is with his admonition in mind that I have written this entire book.